And It Was Very Good

A Latter-day Saint's Guide to Lovemaking

And It Was Very Good

A Latter-day Saint's Guide to Lovemaking

by
Earthly Parents

For our children

Thousands of young people come to the marriage altar almost illiterate insofar as this basic and fundamental function is concerned.

—*Hugh B. Brown*

Parents have primary responsibility for the sex education of their children.

—*Handbook 2: Administering in the Church*

Receive my instruction, and not silver; and knowledge rather than choice gold.

—*Proverbs 8:10*

Our Family's Sexual Articles of Faith

We have written this book for you, our beloved children. As your earthly parents, we have been charged with teaching you about sex. We have been counseled to instruct you "reverently but frankly and without embarrassment."

We hope this book may help you have fulfilling sex lives and avoid misunderstandings that strain too many marriages. We suggest you read this book before your wedding night. You and your spouse may refer back to chapters in the privacy of your home, as you desire. You are past the age where we direct your actions. Instead, consider this book to be advice.

As Latter-day Saints, we raised you to think of sex as a "thou shalt not" before marriage. That was the Lord's direction for you at that time in your life. You have a new commandment in marriage. In marriage, sex is not a barely tolerated necessity of the natural man. In marriage, sex is a "thou shalt."

We declare that God's commandment for His children to multiply and replenish the earth remains in force.... We declare the means by which mortal life is created to be divinely appointed.
—The Family: A Proclamation to the World

As an important part of the expression of their love, the Lord wants a husband and wife to partake of the wonders and joys of marital intimacy.
—Wendy W. Nelson

It's not a suggestion. Embrace what that implies. God wants you to do it. It's right there. Some of us need permission to enjoy something. If that's you, permission granted, from God himself.

Some transitions in life are harder than others. The transition from sexual repression to expression can be difficult. After being raised in a "thou shalt not" phase of life, turning on a dime in marriage can be jarring. Some Latter-day Saints report that sex, even in marriage, feels unclean. Some have their self-worth tied to a premarital denial of sexuality. Some regret a supposed loss of virtue on the wedding night.

As these unfortunate newlyweds move from "thou shalt not" to "thou shalt," they bring the guilty undertones of premarital sex to the marriage bed. They can't quite shake the idea that sex is sin. Some find it hard to let go of the premarital habit of repressing sexual feelings. Those members may struggle to give their spouses the gift of being desired. Some continue a habit of being sexually secretive instead of opening themselves to sexual sharing. Some couples decorate their bedrooms with more shame than pillows. Some couples feel they must choose between sexuality and spirituality.

This is tragic. It's not what God intends for you.

Destructive Sex	Married Sex
"Thou shalt not"	"Thou shalt"
Sinful	Spiritual
Shameful	Joyful
Selfish	Shared
Dirty	Pure
Denying	Desiring
Suppressed	Expressed
Harming	Healing

Don't drag something from here...

...to here!

Other couples find married sex to be joyful. They recognize that sexuality may be a refuge from the world with the right person at the right time. They understand that both husband's and wife's sexualities are God-given gifts to share with the other. These couples recognize that in marriage we will be spiritual *and* sexual. Indeed, these couples realize sexuality may be a deeply spiritual act. We wish this for you.

> Such an act of love between a man and a woman is—or certainly was ordained to be—a symbol of total union: union of their hearts, their hopes, their lives, their love, their family, their future, their everything.
>
> — *Jeffrey R. Holland*

It's worth laying out our fundamental beliefs about married sex. These beliefs seem good and right to us. These beliefs appear to us to have doctrinal support. We have received confirmation from the Spirit that we should pass our beliefs on to you. Don't rely on our faith, of course. We suggest you and your spouse consult with the Spirit and decide in your own hearts if you share our beliefs and if you wish to adopt them in your own family. Our family's "Sexual Articles of Faith" form the foundation upon which we have built our views of sexuality—in this book and in our lives.

We believe sexuality is a good gift from our heavenly parents.

We believe we are literal children of God. Our heavenly parents have gifted us with bodies like unto theirs. These bodies include sexuality in all its wonder. Indeed, if there is any religion on the earth today that may lay claim to a belief in the divinity of sex, it is the gospel of Jesus Christ.

We believe married sex is for joy and bonding in addition to creating new mortal bodies for spirit children to inhabit.

We are that we might have joy—and not just for the life hereafter.

> *...sexual relations within marriage are divinely approved not only for the purpose of procreation, but also as a way of expressing love and strengthening emotional and spiritual bonds between husband and wife.*
>
> —Handbook 2: Administering in the Church

We believe God has ordained sex for the married couple. Nobody else should be involved.

Any sexual intimacy outside of the bonds of marriage—I mean any intentional contact with the sacred, private parts of another's body, with or without clothing—is a sin and is forbidden by God.

—Richard G. Scott

We believe sex is not a right to be demanded but a gift to be offered and received voluntarily.

...a woman should be queen of her own body. The marriage covenant does not give the man the right to enslave her, or to abuse her, or to use her merely for the gratification of his passion. Your marriage ceremony does not give you that right.

—David O. McKay

We believe husbands and wives are individually responsible for expressing their own sexual desires and for caring for each other's sexual needs.

Nobody else can do this for you.

Husband and wife have a solemn responsibility to love and care for each other...
—The Family: A Proclamation to the World

Tenderness and respect—never selfishness—must be the guiding principles in the intimate relationship between husband and wife. Each partner must be considerate and sensitive to the other's needs and desires.
—Howard W. Hunter

We believe viewing pornography is forbidden.

Church leaders warn against viewing sexually explicit images of those outside the marriage. We're not going to recommend viewing pornography, and we won't discuss it except to point out some of its downsides.

We didn't cover all this in family home evening. Rather, we have consciously shielded you prior to now from detailed erotic knowledge. We asked you to wait to date until the age of sixteen. We discouraged exposure to media we believed might tempt you to commit sexual sin. We avoided discussing some intimate details so we would not heighten your sexual feelings when you weren't ready to make good use of them.

Parents ideally teach sexual facts and values. No other source is likely to give you both.

Church instructs on values but few sexual facts. The values taught on Sunday tend toward the "thou shalt not" part. Over the years we've been instructed at least one hundred times on the evils of pornography and exactly zero times on techniques of sexual pleasure. Church members are human and may pass on false traditions. It's our observation that false teachings among fellow Latter-day Saints tend toward negative framing of God-given sexuality and normal sexual behavior that might bless a marriage. Well-meaning people sometimes pass on rules that don't exist.

We don't expect school to have taught you gospel values about sex. We don't even expect school sex education to have given you the useful facts. Some sex-ed classes focus on menstrual cycles and puberty while skipping the how-to bits. How to find the clitoris in the dark probably wasn't on the quiz.

The internet has the facts somewhere out there, of course. Unfortunately, keyword searches practically guarantee you will see porn. That's just the reality. Plus, the internet is full of nonsense.

The magazines you see in the grocery checkout line are the worst. They just make stuff up. It's easier to make up a quote than it is to interview an expert. It's easier to make up statistics than it is to look up an actual study.

Sex manuals are better. However, far too many are thinly veiled pornography. Even if you do come across an accurate, non-salacious sex manual, the framing may be counter to gospel principles.

Here, we've chosen facts and advice from select

manuals, expert-hosted podcasts, and academic journals. We have avoided the outright pornographic nature of some sources and have steered clear of that which is in direct conflict with unambiguous gospel teachings.

That's not to say you or your spouse will read this and necessarily think we've drawn the line at the right place. Where God is silent on what exactly is fulfilling the law of chastity, we're not filling in the blanks for you. We can't. Married sex is actually one of the least rule-bound areas of the gospel. It's largely left to you and your spouse to work out how to use your sexuality to bless each other. Perhaps married sex is an area where God has decided it is not meet that we be commanded in all things.

Along those lines, there is no doctrine of which we are aware governing whose hand does what during married sexual activity. That's not an endorsement but an honest admission. This one is up to you, your spouse, and the Lord.

This gets us to our family's seventh and last Sexual Article of Faith.

We believe sex that unites a married couple in Christ is good and sex that divides a married couple is bad.

God intends the married couple to "become as one." Sex can be a glorious means to this end. A faithful Latter-day Saint couple may study in their own minds (and bodies!) if this or that sexual act is good or bad given their unique circumstances. A first test can be "does this act unite us or divide us?" Sex that unites a couple may accomplish the will of the Lord. Sex that divides a couple cannot.

Now is the right time. Here is what we feel you should know.

EARTHLY PARENTS

It was hard to move away from the thought that sex was something dirty that you were to not talk about—to it is now allowed and indeed even encouraged as a form of bonding and coming closer to one another.

—Latter-day Saint wife, married at 23

As a former bishop who counseled couples pre and post wedding, I've encouraged them to not simply rule anything out because of perceived culture. If they are both comfortable with it and want to try something, go for it.

—Latter-day Saint husband, married at 22

Sexual Hunger (Libido)

Sex is as essential to mortal life as food. Hunger reminds us we are missing something vital. If we've eaten, we can focus on tasks that require our attention. If we are hungry, we get cranky. If we are starving, we can be mean.

What do we do if we are hungry? We prepare a meal. We eat.

We've eaten food our whole lives. We know how to eat food. We know how to think about eating food. We know some like pasta. Some like steak. Some even like Brussel sprouts. Some prefer set meals. Some want to eat whenever. Some try a different dish at every restaurant. Some have old favorites they order again and again.

When it comes to sex, it can be easy to forget the lessons our bellies have already taught us. We can get annoyed, angry, or plain weirded out. We'd do well to remember the lessons we've already learned from a lifetime of eating.

Some people have big (sexual) appetites. Other people have small (sexual) appetites. That's okay. Some people want a variety of (sexual) dishes for different meals. Other people want only one (sexual) dish most of the time. That's okay. Sometimes we prepare a (sexual) meal that someone else loves. Sometimes we cook up a (sexual) meal that's not to the liking of another. That's also okay.

Do we flip out when we are hungry and our spouse isn't? No! Do we feel bad when our spouse wants pizza...again? No! Do we beat ourselves up if our spouse just can't stand the thought of sushi? Of course, we don't.

If you and your spouse are going to have fights about sex, it's most likely going to be over differences in sexual hunger. It's impossible for you both to have the same, exact sexual appetites. You won't like exactly the same things. You won't want exactly the same amounts. There will always be a higher-desire spouse and a lower-desire spouse at any one time in a marriage. The guaranteed difference in sexual appetites can tear a marriage apart if you let it. Don't.

A desire difference will never be eliminated. Expect it. It's normal.

If you are sexually hungry more often than your spouse is, that's okay. It doesn't say anything bad about you or your spouse. That doesn't say anything bad at all. Your spouse doesn't love you less. Your spouse just isn't hungry yet. You have the responsibility to express your sexual hunger if your spouse doesn't know. Just don't be a jerk about it even if you are feeling really hungry. Sometimes it's not a good time for your spouse to feed you. Sometimes there is only time for a sexual snack rather than a full meal.

If you don't feel sexual hunger as often or intensely as your spouse does, that's also okay. If your spouse is hungry and wants to eat, that doesn't mean your spouse is selfish. That doesn't mean your spouse is more loving or more committed to the marriage. It means your spouse is hungry. Even if you are not hungry, your spouse may need to eat. You might not be ready to eat a full meal. Maybe a sexual snack will tide your spouse over until you are also hungry.

A considerate spouse will communicate sexual hunger honestly and seek to feed his or her spouse's sexual hunger. However, failure of a husband or wife to be sexually considerate bestows no right to sex on a spouse. Sexuality is a gift to be shared, not a right to be demanded. Sexual hunger is much like food hunger in this. Being hungry does not bestow the right to eat whatever one wants.

Nonetheless, marriage—especially in light of gospel teachings on procreation—is not merely a really close friendship. Marriage is an agreement to be in an intimate, exclusive, *sexual* relationship. Sex is an essential part of the plan, circumstances permitting. Denying a spouse's sexual hunger as a form of control or punishment is cruel. Withholding from the hungry when one has a full pantry is the stuff of Charles Dickens.

When a married couple is open and honest about their sexual hunger, it's easier for both to be fed properly. Open communication is essential, or spouses naturally assume the other may share the same hunger pangs. It's also important to be honest about sexual hunger, or trust breaks down.

Some spouses exaggerate sexual hunger or intentionally inflame it at inopportune times. These spouses may be seeking to add to a ledger of supposed sexual debt to be withdrawn upon demand. First of all, there is no sexual debt ever. Nobody owes sex to anyone. Second, exaggerating a debt is theft—even supposing such a debt existed. Third, any effort to cash in a sexual debt to buy a loving, passionate experience will backfire. Duty sex is a chore. Duty sex kills desire. If we were to feign constant starvation, our spouses would sooner or later dread cooking. Exaggerating sexual hunger to gain sympathy or control is a form of unrighteous dominion.

Other spouses deliberately repress their own sexual hunger. Suppressing sexual hunger when it would bless a spouse is no virtue. Libido denial may be a way to withhold full commitment to a marriage. If every time we made a meal our spouse pretended not to be interested in food, it would hurt us. We all have the sexual need to be needed.

Thinking about food can make us hungry. Laying out a meal helps some people realize they haven't eaten for a while. Seeing and smelling a big Thanksgiving spread with turkey and buttered rolls can make our mouths water. Sexual hunger is also like that. Some people don't feel sexual hunger until they find themselves in a sexual situation. It's not that they don't like sex. They just don't think about it until they realize, "That feels nice. I think I'd like to have some more of that." They like sex...but forget they like it. Their desire is responsive. Waiting for a spouse with responsive desire to initiate sex can be demoralizing. It can be a long wait.

Instead, the higher-desire spouse can be the one to remember for the couple when it's time to head off to the bedroom. Neither husband nor wife need get put off when only one spouse remembers to get hungry. So long as both enjoy sex once it starts, it's wonderful that someone has a biological alarm clock to chime for them both.

Sexual snacks can keep a hungry spouse going. Sexual snacks are anything sexual that's quick. Quickies are the trail mix of marriage.

Another option to consider is scheduling sex. This may seem too calculated for passion, but scheduled sex can work for couples with large differences in sexual hunger. "Hot date night" seems better than letting a spouse starve. Knowing there is a meal coming up helps the hungry endure. A planned sex night can also help a lower-desire spouse work up an appetite anticipating the upcoming sexual feast.

Thinking about sexual hunger in terms of food hunger makes it easier to share sexuality without upsetting a spouse or becoming upset. In some ways, sexual hunger is the most familiar feeling in the world.

To be turned on, for me, is indescribable feelings of love and appreciation for my spouse. Being turned on makes me feel so good, and so I want to share that with my wife.
—Latter-day Saint husband, married at 28

It is an energy or desire to be closer. Libido isn't just about sex. It is about having an energy and drive in all aspects of life to move forward with and become closer to your eternal companion and God.
—Latter-day Saint wife, married at 20

Sex Parking Brake

Every sexually mature child of God has not one but two sexual arousal systems. These two systems act as a gas pedal and a parking brake. These two systems have technical names: the sexual excitation system and the sexual inhibition system. The push and pull of these two arousal systems helps us have sex only with the right person in the right place at the right time.

We're going to call these two systems the sex gas pedal and the sex parking brake.

Everyone has a sex parking brake. The sex parking brake is what's engaged if sex is a bad idea. The sex parking brake keeps us from feeling sexual with the wrong person or in the wrong place or at the wrong time.

Want to feel your own sex parking brake slam on? Think about having sex with your spouse. Get a bit of a buzz. Then imagine your bedroom door banging open and someone barging in. How do you feel now? *Yikes.* The sex parking brake can bring sexuality to zero mph in a screech.

People don't usually feel sexual towards a near

relative who is objectively attractive. Why not? This is the sex parking brake. Don't feel erotic while giving a church talk? Sex parking brake. Thinking of all the things you have to do before tomorrow, and it's getting late, and money is tight, and you still have the lesson to prepare? Sex parking brake. You get the picture. The sex parking brake helps us avoid inappropriate sex.

The sex parking brake is supposed to release so that we can hit the sex gas pedal and get where we want to go. Guess what? The sex parking brake doesn't always release when we want. You and your spouse will probably have different sensitivities for each of your sex parking brakes. It's like some cars. Our Odyssey has a parking brake with a release pull that is easy to flip. Our Toyota's parking brake takes some effort to unclench.

For some people—this is more often true of husbands—the sex parking brake is easy to release. It may not take much to ignore the cares of the world, to disengage the sex parking brake. The couple may not have to invest energy releasing his sex parking brake when it's time to have sex.

For other people—and this is more often true of wives—the sex parking brake can get stuck. You are in the right place and time for sex with the right person, but you can't stop thinking about other things. Maybe you are thinking about paying the rent. Maybe you are thinking about how your spouse was angry at you the other day. You can't focus. Maybe your spouse is getting frustrated that you aren't into it. As your spouse accuses you of not being into it, your sex parking brake clamps down. Now *you're* angry. The car is at a dead stop in the driveway.

Now, husbands, do you know why you might need to start the laundry before your wife is into sex? It's her sex parking brake.

The first part of sex happens before the bedroom. There is a process to releasing the sex parking brake. To the extent a wife needs her parking brake released, that's job one. (It's usually the woman's sex parking brake that needs to be released.) Just knowing her sex parking brake is there can be a great help. Husbands and wives both should take responsibility for releasing her sex parking brake.

Men, learn what distracts your wife from sex. If it's a household chore that needs to be done, do it. A couple from our stake calls this choreplay. If your wife has a backache, give her a massage. If she is distracted by neighbors' voices, turn on some music. If she is worried about the kids coming in, check the door lock *while she is watching.* Remove distractions. Make your sex space a safe space. Help release her sex parking brake. This is not wasted time. This is sex.

Women, to the extent that you need to have your own sex parking brake released, plan for it. Think in advance of your distractors and check the items off your list or ask your spouse to do what you just know will bug you if it remains undone. Don't take on an extra project at the eleventh hour if you know it will distract you at midnight. If your feet get cold, wear socks. Don't beat yourself up that you can't get into sex until things are settled. Releasing your sex parking brake is necessary. It's what you need. This is sex.

There is another way the sex parking brake can get stuck. During sex, we may find ourselves ensnared in negative self-talk. Negative thoughts may turn us from a participant who is lost in the moment to a critical observer. "Am I attractive? What is my face doing? Do I look funny?" This self-talk could derail anyone from having a satisfying sexual encounter.

In men, this kind of sex parking brake can lead to erectile dysfunction. "What if I can't keep it up? What will she think of me? I bet she wishes she had a real man." Of course, these negative thoughts can lead to a loss of arousal.

In women, sexual performance anxiety can make it hard for her to focus. "Why do I take so long to orgasm? Am I broken?" These negative thoughts can make orgasm impossible for a woman. The sex parking brake can be a self-fulfilling doomsday prophecy.

When the sex parking brake is stuck because of negative self-talk, a recommended solution is mindfulness. Negative thoughts can gain purchase when we let our minds wander. Attending to sex—paying attention to what one is doing, feeling, seeing, hearing, smelling—can give negative thoughts no place to enter. Being in the moment focuses us on arousing sensations and lets the sex parking brake stay safely released. We'll talk more about focusing the mind in the "Touching Her" chapter.

Reading up about sex may also help. Realistic expectations lower performance anxiety. Learning that one is normal, or at least has a lot of company, tends to put anyone at ease.

It can be thrilling to step on the sex gas pedal, but you only get there if the sex parking brake is off.

I had had the problem where I'd trained down my libido a lot in order to stay chaste, so I've had to reactivate it since being married.
—Latter-day Saint husband, married at 31

I was way too uptight and felt like if I explored too much or enjoyed too much it would be a sin.
—Latter-day Saint wife, married at 23

What Women Want

Sexually speaking, some things are the same between men and women. God has gifted us with bodies that are much more alike than different. We all have brains, skin, nerves, and erogenous zones. We all are sexual beings and have been so from before birth—body and spirit. The brain is the main sex organ for both men and women. Male and female brains share form and parts. Arousal, pleasure seeking, reward, and pair bonding are built upon the same neurochemical pathways. Our genitals are made from the same embryonic stuff. It makes sense that many sexual things feel the same to each of us, male and female.

Orgasm, the joyful climax of sexual response, may feel the same for both men and women. When men and women describe orgasm with gender-specific words stripped out, readers can't figure out who said what. Male and female brains have similar activities during orgasm when imaged by PET and fMRI scans.

Our own body is our first guide to a spouse's sexual response. Our bodies are not *expert* guides, to be sure, but they know the basic lay of the land. We find what feels good to us and try that or the closest thing to it with our spouse. "What's good for me is good for you" works for many sexual touches. Our bodies are more alike than different in what feels physically pleasurable.

That's the upside of doing what our bodies know. The downside is that what feels good to her might feel lousy to him, and vice versa. Our body is a novice guide that can get lost when it leaves the familiar path. Some things are different, sexually, between genders and from person to person.

As the adage goes, "It ain't what you don't know that gets you into trouble. It's what you know for sure that just ain't so."

Some of us try what we have seen on television or the movies. TV and movies show statistically improbable sex or things that just don't work. Porn can really give the wrong ideas. Physical positioning in porn works for cameras but not real life. Porn timing is not real-sex timing. Over-the-top sexual responses depicted in porn set a viewer up for disappointment and insecurity.

Some of us try what we have heard from friends or family, often based on what worked in their own relationships. Those who have had prior sexual experience try what worked for a past sexual partner. Experience gained with one partner may be the wrong guide to another's sexual ins and outs. Different women have different nerve arrangements in their pelvis and different touch preferences. What was 100% right for a prior sex partner may be 100% wrong with a wife.

Each person is different, and we have to be ready to throw away things we know for sure that just ain't so.

Don't worry. Our role is not to be experts on everyone. We are called to serve one person. It's a pleasure to put in the "10,000 hours" becoming the virtuoso, best-in-world player of our spouse's sexual instrument. We have a lifetime to do it.

You've done the choreplay. You've minimized distractions. The sex parking brake is off. The wife is ready to give feedback on what feels good. The husband is ready to pay attention. Where do we go now?

Are there warm-up activities that sound nice to her? Does she want to kiss? Does she want to cuddle? He should do those things. Does she want the lights on or off? Does she want to be undressed or to undress herself? Slowly or quickly? While he watches or under the covers? He should do that.

This is as good a time as any to say what they hint at in the temple but don't say outright. We take our temple garments off for sex. If the wife wants, she can put on different underwear she finds sexy. She may find it erotic to have her husband fully dressed or wearing particular items of clothing. She may want him to be nude except for his garments. She may want them both to be naked from the start. Focusing on what she wants during her turn to receive pleasure is a good way to go.

Those new to sex don't quite know what they

want. If we haven't done it, we just don't know. This is going to be an exploration. If the wife can give directions, that's great. If she doesn't yet know her own sexual preferences or finds giving directions to be a distraction, then it's going to be trial and error to figure out what works best for her. That's okay.

With direct feedback, a husband can learn more quickly what works for his wife. Using words can be effective, but there is some evidence that nonverbal cues are associated with greater sexual pleasure. A moan is a near-universal sign of "that feels good." Short words may allow her to maintain her focus. *No, yes*, and *ow* get the point across.

The husband can also watch for physical signs of his wife's sexual arousal. These signs may include deeper or faster breathing, muscle jerks, skin flush on her face and chest, muscle tension, puffing lips, twitching face, elevated heart rate, and arteries visibly pulsing. Her breasts may swell. Her nipples may darken and become erect then appear to be less erect as her areolas (the colored rings surrounding her nipples) swell around her nipples. Her labia are likely to darken and swell with blood. She may lick her lips or rub her face as she approaches orgasm. These are imperfect signs. Some physical reactions say that she is feeling *something* but may not indicate whether it's a good or bad feeling. Direct feedback will be more reliable.

A basic pattern to arousing a female is to start everywhere but the genitals and work your way there. She may like her back scratched right away.

She may like to be kissed early on and to be touched on her face and ears after that. Lightly brushing the skin of her outer thighs then inner thighs may feel good to her. And so on. Her breasts may take longer to be receptive. Her nipples may be the last part of her breasts that enjoy touch, and she may never want them touched at all. Her genitals may take twenty minutes or more to be ready for touch.

Anticipation of sexual touch can be exciting. Moving close to an erogenous zone and then away can be arousing.

Some women like their breasts caressed. Some women don't. Breast size means nothing about how much a woman enjoys breast play. As a wife becomes aroused, having her breasts touched or kissed may be exciting to her. A husband can try brushing lightly around the perimeter of his wife's breasts and work his way in toward the areola. Eventually, he may directly touch her nipples if she wants that. She may not. Nipples can be sensitive. He may be drawn to touching her nipples before she is ready. Women report wanting gentler kneading or cupping of the full breast than men choose if left to their own devices. At different points in a sex session, she may want different parts of her breasts touched. Or not. What feels good to her at one moment may be too much at another. Breast sensitivity also changes with hormones.

Everything but everything depends on what she enjoys at the time. There are no hard and fast rules other than "pay attention" as he moves among her erogenous zones toward the last one: her vulva.

"Wait," some of you are saying. "Vulva? Not vagina?" We'll need a female anatomy lesson. That's next.

It's not selfish to ask for what you want. As a wife, sex is not your duty to please your husband whenever he wants. Your sexual desires matter too.

—Latter-day Saint wife, married at 25

I didn't know anything about my sexual response (aside from what I learned from heavy make out sessions).

—Latter-day Saint wife, married at 20

What's Down There

Mark Twain wrote, "The difference between the almost right word and the right word is really a large matter—it's the difference between the lightning bug and the lightning."

Many of us use vague or just plain wrong words to describe the female genitalia. It's common to use the word *vagina* for the whole thing. It's not. The vagina is one part. "Down there" and "pee area" can make it seem gross. Dismissive words can demean a place of pleasure that is the wellspring of life itself.

Genitals have parts, and each part has a name. Women, you can get a hand mirror and give yours a look. If you have avoided this until now, it's past time to do it. The more know about yourself, the better you will be at helping your husband learn what you want, sexually. Men, pay attention. You need to know this.

The whole outer part that you can see when you look "down there" is a woman's **vulva**. Above her vulva is pubic hair on a mound of flesh and subcutaneous fat. That mound is called her *mons veneris* (mound of Venus) or just **mons**.

Vulva

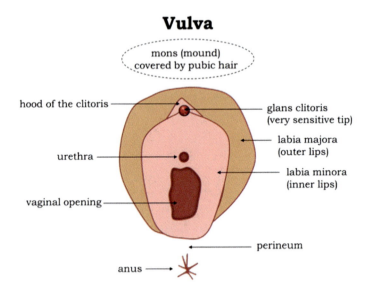

Husbands, you are going to want to know that part. On a man, the area may be more of a random spot of tissue than an erotic zone. Some women are different. Her *mons* may be one of her sexual hot zones.

Below a woman's *mons* are two lips of flesh. These are her **outer labia** (literally "lips"). Between her outer labia, you may see some crinkly skin. These softer lips are her **inner labia**. Having these touched can feel good to her when she is ready. There is huge variation in normal labia size and shape. Some inner labia are fully enclosed by the outer labia. Some inner labia protrude and may be larger than the outer labia. Asymmetry is the norm. Labia are like orchids: Each one is unique. Labia size and shape do not predict how she will

Clitoris Below the Surface

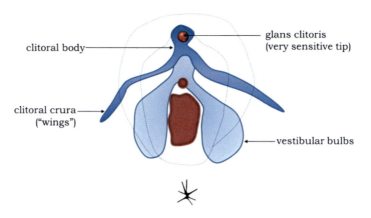

clitoral body

glans clitoris
(very sensitive tip)

clitoral crura
("wings")

vestibular bulbs

like to be touched or how much she will enjoy sex.

Below the top of the "split" of a woman's outer labia is something that should probably not be touched right away because it's very sensitive. There is a bump of flesh—it could be fingertip-sized and poke out or a tiny nib that's hidden—called the **glans clitoris**. This part is the same type of tissue as the head of the penis. Husbands, you know how your penis feels good if it's touched there in the right way and "not good at all, ouch!" if it's touched in the wrong way? Your wife's clitoris has more nerve endings than your entire penis. The clitoris is *concentrated.* Her clitoris will probably be too sensitive for direct touch until she is sexually aroused.

The clitoris has only one known function:

female sexual pleasure. Two thirds of women prefer direct clitoral stimulation at the right time during sexual activity. Most women also enjoy stimulation near the clitoris. Two-thirds of surveyed women who self-stimulate will at times stimulate the clitoris indirectly through nearby labial tissue or even light cloth.

Wait! husbands. Don't touch your wife's clitoris with a dry hand. It will irritate her. She has to be ready for touch and will probably need natural or commercial lubrication for your touch to be pleasurable.

The top of a woman's clitoris is covered by a hood of flesh. The *glans clitoris* pokes out of this hood at times and retracts at others. How much the clitoris protrudes depends on the woman and her level of sexual excitement.

Below the *glans clitoris* is the external end of the **urethra** ("pee hole"). It may feel good to a woman to have this area stimulated. The doughnut-shaped ring of flesh surrounding her urethral opening may puff visibly when she is aroused.

Below a wife's urethra is the opening to her **vagina**. This is where her husband's penis goes at the right time.

Notice how we said the *glans clitoris* when we talked about the bump? Most of the time we call this the clitoris, but in reality the entire clitoris is not merely the *glans*. A woman's whole clitoris is about as large as a penis. Really. Only the very tip of her clitoris may peek out to the world. The rest of her clitoris extends internally in a winged wishbone shape. Her *glans* connects to her clitoral body, which connects to her pubic bone. Her clitoral structure extends along her pubic bone in "wings" called *crura.* Her clitoris also has vestibular bulbs that reach around the top and sides of her vagina.

As a wife becomes sexually stimulated, her vestibular bulbs will engorge with blood in a way that's similar to a penile erection. This engorgement is internal and less obvious than an erection. Female genital engorgement does not cause penis-like stiffness. Instead, her vascular tissue is spongy. Her engorged vestibular bulbs swell around her vagina and press on the top and sides of her vaginal opening.

This swelling is mostly hidden. Hidden things are sometimes important. This hidden thing is a treasure. Vestibular bulb swelling will cause her vagina to release lubrication. Her sexual excitement increases along with that swelling. Movement in parts of her vulva that are far from the tip of the clitoris—say, by a finger or penis in her vagina—may be transmitted through the internal parts of her engorged clitoris to her sensitive nerve endings in her *glans.*

The clitoris is the most important sexual stimulation point for a woman. If she orgasms, her clitoris will likely have been touched erotically for twenty minutes or more.

My husband had no idea what a woman's body was like. I had to give him an anatomy lesson.
    —*Latter-day Saint wife, married at 28*

She and I never talked about sex before marriage. Wish I knew where and what a clitoris was, and she basically didn't even know what she looked like down there either.
    —*Latter-day Saint husband, married at 21*

Her Turn

The sexual response cycle for both men and women goes from excitement, to plateau, to orgasm, to resolution. The most obvious difference between male and female sexual response can be summed up in one word: time. The erect penis can be ready to orgasm in seconds or minutes. Women usually take longer. Some sources have popularized a "20-20 rule" for women: Twenty minutes of nongenital touch followed by twenty minutes of genital touch. Every woman is different though. Some women can orgasm in five minutes. Some women require over an hour.

Both male and female genitals engorge with blood as sexual excitement builds. There are one-way valves that allow blood to fill chambers that give the penis rigidity. For women, the valves are leakier. Female erectile tissue acts more like a sponge that's filling up and dripping at the same time. Her tissues swell with her sexual excitement, but the swelling is not immediate and can reverse. Stop stimulating a man, and he may remain erect. Stop stimulating a woman, and she can lose the

Female Sexual Response Cycle

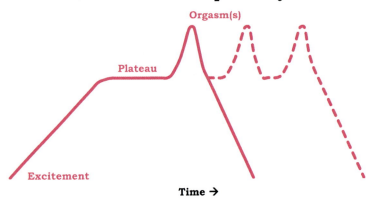

progress she's made building her sexual excitement. Her engorged tissues require steady stimulation not to drain of blood and drain her arousal with it.

One fun part of the female sexual response cycle is that she gets to enjoy a slow build to peak sexual excitement, and her lover gets to enjoy watching her arousal for a long time.

The 99.9% reality is this: If a husband puts his penis in the moment it feels good to go from his perspective, it's almost never going to be the right time for his wife. Female sexual response is a process. Savor it.

Wife's Plan: If a wife wants her husband to do something, she should tell him or show him. If he's a bit off the mark, the most loving words a wife can say are *left* or *right*, *higher* or *lower*, *faster* or *slower*. Husbands aren't mind readers. If it feels good, she should let him know. The three little words everyone wants to hear during sex are "I like that." If what he's doing feels bad, she should *really* let him know...kindly. A bit of tact can go a long way. "What I think I'd like instead..." is less likely to wound than "that's really bad."

Husband's Plan: A husband should pay attention to his wife. If she says she wants something, he should do it. If she says it feels bad, he should cut it out. Follow directions.

What feels good to a wife will change with hormones and during a sexual encounter. A responsive husband will follow directions and do what is right for her at the time. A couple can't go too far wrong if she tells him what she wants and he does what she asks. They can use this plan to move from what feels good now to what feels good next for her entire sexual response cycle.

If a husband keeps doing what feels erotic to his wife, her arousal will build. Touch outside her genitals will prepare her genitals to become receptive. Her vulva will begin to engorge with blood. After about twenty minutes or more of nongenital erotic touch, her genitals may find his touch to be pleasurable.

Parts that felt wrong to be touched at the beginning may feel right to be touched later on, and then "very much right." The area around and possibly directly on her clitoris tip may enjoy rhythmic stroking. Her inner labia will puff and noticeably darken. The vestibular bulbs of her clitoris will engorge and press on the top and sides of her vagina. Her ability to feel pain will go down.

Her vagina will lengthen by about half and release lubricant to become ready to welcome a penis. Her expanding tissue may engulf the *glans* of her clitoris, which may seem to hide.

The wife's engorged clitoris will receive stimulation from nearby touch and pressure. A tug of her inner labia, a rub of her vaginal opening, a push on her *mons* may each get transferred to her large, hidden clitoral structure. It can all feel good.

After time, the wife will reach a plateau of sexual excitement, where her pleasure can be intense. Plateau is many people's favorite sexual state. If she is experienced with orgasm, she may seek to prolong the time she spends at her sexual plateau.

With continued stimulation at plateau, the wife's climax point may be reached. Past this point, her nervous system will fire in a sexual feedback called an orgasm. Saying orgasm is enjoyable is an understatement. Orgasm feels *fantastic.*

With orgasm the wife's blood pressure will spike. Her pelvic muscles will start to clench and release. Her orgasmic spasms will include her uterus. Her face may adopt a look of pain even while she feels pleasure. Her toes may reflexively curl up except her big toe, which may stick out. She may feel the urge to moan. Her brain may go into a semi-dream state of altered consciousness. Orgasmic contractions will pulse through her in waves. These contractions may be irregular, or she may have regular waves at 0.8 second intervals.

She may have regular contractions followed by irregular shudders. Her orgasm will last about ten to thirty seconds. This may seem shorter to her orgasmic brain, which may lose track of time. Her face and torso may develop a temporary rash-like sexual flush. Endorphins will flood her blood as her brain rewards her for sex and bonds her to her husband.

Some women may orgasm a second time or more if they continue to receive stimulation. There is no known limit to the number of orgasms some women can have in one session.

And then it's time to be done with stimulation. The wife may want to cuddle. She may want to talk and connect with her husband. She may wish to bond with intercourse. Her need to connect driven in part by the release of the pair-bonding hormone oxytocin.

If you are reading this and haven't yet had an orgasm, we promise it's not a myth. Orgasm isn't something *Teen Vogue* made up. Orgasm is real, and 95% of women (eventually) find this pearl of great price hidden in their God-given bodies. We'll talk more about how a woman may to learn to orgasm the "Misfires" chapter.

Sex feels really good, and it's really enjoyable for both partners. It took about a month to figure that out.

—Latter-day Saint wife, married at 22

It took me twenty years to realize the key for the majority of women is clitoral stimulation.

—Latter-day Saint husband, married at 30

Touching Her

"Ladies first" isn't just for lifeboats. Because women take longer to reach orgasm, delaying his orgasm until she has had her turn can benefit both husband and wife. The other way round can also work if he remembers to be attentive to her needs after his have been met.

Orgasm need not be her goal. Many women find sexual activity without orgasm to be satisfying. Another reason to be less goal-oriented is that without the pressure of achieving orgasm, her orgasm becomes more likely.

After twenty minutes or so of nongenital touch, she may be ready to have her vulva touched. But with what? What should a husband use to stimulate his wife? The no-hands, simultaneous orgasm we see in the movies is misleading. Her orgasm may come by hand (probably), mouth (likely), vibrator (reliably), or penis (not so much).

Sexual stimulation of a woman without intercourse is usually called foreplay. Foreplay is a word that frames sex from the male perspective. For women, foreplay isn't just the appetizer before

How Women Orgasm

Yes but *never* during intercourse

25% *Some of the time* during intercourse

25% *Most of the time* during intercourse

5% No orgasm yet

the main meal. For most women, foreplay *is* sex.

This is important. Intercourse is for the most part a male mode of sexual behavior. Most women report *never* having an orgasm by intercourse alone. Those women who do orgasm during intercourse usually need additional, direct stimulation to the clitoris. Someone will have a hand down there to rub her clitoris or position a vibrator during intercourse.

Even if she is able to orgasm from penis alone, there is going to be a lot of touching before insertion is likely to feel pleasurable to her.

Eventually, she may want him to move his hand down to her vulva. Light brushing will probably feel good before anything more direct.

The wife has one act her husband cannot do for her. *She has to feel good on purpose.* If something feels sexy to her, she will need to accept the feeling. She can't turn it off. She has to allow herself to be turned on. Feeling erotic is something she will have to welcome in.

Erotic feelings may have felt wrong or dirty prior to marriage. In marriage, erotic feelings are not wrong. They are right. Sexuality is not dirty—it's just different. Sexuality is a weird and wonderful birthright given to each of us from our loving heavenly parents.

Both wife and husband each have been gifted their own unique erotic capacity to be opened up and shared with the other. Marriage is the right time to explore and wonder at each other's sexual gifts together. The sexual gift is a living thing that can seem to have a will of its own.

For a wife to share her sexual gift with her husband, she will have to choose to crack open the gift box and see what thoughts her sexuality likes to be fed. For most women, only when fed these thoughts will her sexuality come out and run free.

To build erotic feelings, the wife will most likely need to focus her thoughts on what is sexy to her. She should take an active mental role. It may be exciting to think about exactly what she and her husband are doing at that moment. If she finds it arousing to think about where and how she is being touched, she may think it and keep thinking it. Mindfulness can enhance sex.

More commonly, the wife will kindle her arousal by visualizing romantic scenes or erotic situations. Most women have to focus on a vivid or story-like scenario to build their sexual excitement to the point of orgasm.

These scenes can be memories of past romantic

or sexual acts. These scenes can be about things the wife has read. These scenes can be complete fantasy. These scenes can be things she would like to do or things she would never want to experience in real life. Each woman will find her own scenes that work for her. A wife can try different scenes to see which ones her sexual self likes best.

The most common settings for favorite imagined scenes are semi-public, where the couple may be caught in the act. These semi-public spaces include elevators, offices, locker rooms, and parks. Imagining fear of exposure triggers heavy breathing and a racing heart. Where else do we breathe heavily with a racing heart? Sex. A semi-public sex scene may trick our bodies into physical arousal that can turn into sexual arousal.

Other settings have a different purpose. Imagining romantic situations where there isn't a care in the world may help a wife relax and access her sexuality. The most common romantic settings where women stage their favorite scenes are, in order, at the beach, in nature, and in the shower.

Romantic scenes may fill an emotional need. Women may focus on being loved, cared for, and especially sexually desired. Exciting scenes may involve being an irresistible object of male desire. She may find imagining a man losing control over her to be thrilling.

Some women find authority scenes work best. Authority scenes where the woman must perform sexually for an authority figure may help her overcome lingering, premarital guilt over her sexual feelings. A wife may project herself into a scene where she imagines her husband to be an authority figure such as a doctor examining her or a police officer in uniform who has to be obeyed for her to get out of a ticket. These scenes may allow her to accept sexual pleasure. In her fantasy scene, she may secretly enjoy what she is ordered to do, but she isn't responsible for the sexual activity.

Each wife will have to learn which thoughts she finds most erotic. Thinking of her sexuality as a living thing with its own wants and needs may allow her to become comfortable with giving her sexuality the romantic or erotic scenes that will make it thrive.

Of note, some women find scenes of compelled sex to be arousing. This may be true even though in real life they would never want sex to be compelled. Some women have been raised to believe sexual feelings are unacceptable or unfeminine and find it difficult in marriage to access their own eroticism. Imagining being forced into receiving sexual pleasure can provide the permission a woman needs to build her sexual excitement. These scenes may enable her arousal despite an excessively repressive upbringing or even sexual trauma. Viewed in that light, even scenes involving compulsion can be useful to a woman and ultimately bless her marriage.

If the wife's favorite scenes do not disturb her, there is nothing she need worry about. Some women, however, are disturbed by what scenes they find arousing. Exploring the reasons behind the need for a disturbing scene may sap it of its disturbing nature. A woman whose preferred scenes disturb her can start with a tried-and-true scene before moving on to other scenes that are more acceptable to her. Counseling from a certified sex therapist may help her understand herself and expand what turns her on.

The wife will think her erotic thoughts while her husband touches her erogenous zones including her genitals. The touch that feels best to her will likely be teasing and light at the beginning. He can start with light brushing of her *mons*, outer labia, and inner thighs. Stress on *light*. He probably will have to be gentler than he ever would be in handling his own genitals.

Gradually, the husband can begin to rub his wife's vulva with more pressure. She may like moderate pressure and a grinding feeling against her vulva. She may enjoy a cupping of her *mons* and outer labia in a "vulva hug." To do this, he will place the heel of his palm on her *mons* and use his fingers to cup her outer labia. He will grip or hug her vulva for a few seconds, release, then repeat.

As the wife gets sexually excited, her vagina will become moist. Natural vaginal lubrication signals the *start* of her sexual receptivity, though, not the end of the process. Vaginal wetness does not mean that she is about to orgasm or that it's time for penile penetration. So stand down, men.

Light finger pressure on the inner labia can start to feel good after brushing the outer lips and hugging or grinding on the vulva. The husband will eventually tease apart his wife's inner labia. This is a delicate moment. Dry fingers chafe.

Fingernails should be trimmed. Calluses can hurt.

The solution is lubrication. He may dip a finger into the opening of her vagina and pull up some natural lube. Or he can use a water-based or silicone-based lubricant. Saliva can work for a bit but dries up and must be reapplied. Some recommend coconut oil, but all oil-based lubricants degrade latex and should not be used with condoms. His lubricated finger can rub her inner labia and eventually the area near her clitoris.

Which exact spot to rub nobody can know except for the woman. What feels good may move around. One spot can get overstimulated or numb. Motions that feel good can be up and down, circular, back and forth, or whatever she likes. Her preferred focus is probably going to be below her clitoris tip and above her vaginal opening. Touching her above her clitoral hood could also be enjoyable.

There will be a rhythm and range of motion that feels best at the time to her. The most common preference reported is up and down with light or medium pressure. Nearly half of women prefer one motion exclusively. Sticking to a motion that feels good will help build her excitement. This may take a while. Enjoy it.

If you are both new to this and it's not feeling good, that's okay. You can stop and do something else. A husband has a lifetime to learn his wife's needs. A wife has a lifetime to learn how to think sexy thoughts.

Eventually, it may feel better to be more direct

on her clitoral *glans*. Or it may never, ever, ever, *ever* feel right to touch the sensitive clitoral *glans* directly. Different women are different.

Husbands have two hands and a mouth. He should use them. His wife may enjoy a symphony of stimulations while she is being pleasured by hand. She may like to have her face touched. She may want to be kissed. She may want her breasts kissed or massaged. She may like her ears or neck brushed. Or she may want complete focus on her vulva.

As the woman gets more excited, she may enjoy having a finger or fingers inserted in her vagina. Here is where guys tend to get it wrong. What sounds good to a man, sexually, is probably thrusting a penis in and out and going deep. If she likes that exact in-out motion deep in her vagina, she's in the minority. So listen up, men.

There are relatively few nerves deep in a woman's vagina. After all, the vagina may eventually birth a baby. Her pleasure nerves are routed away from the birth canal and possible trauma of childbirth. The deepest two-thirds of the vagina may be unable to feel anything but pressure. If something does push all the way to her cervix (the opening of her womb), it may not feel good to her at all. It may just hurt. From her perspective, the pleasure will probably be in the first third of her vagina. These are the places the engorged interior clitoral structures contact.

With that in mind, the husband can spend some time at the opening of his wife's vagina. She may like him to circle a finger around the opening.

She may like him to push into the vaginal opening until it clenches and then relaxes. She may like a bit of a stretching feeling of fingers pressing against the sides of her vaginal opening. Stimulating the outer third of the vagina tends to engage the pudendal nerve, which is a sexual pleasure nerve second only to the pelvic nerve that innervates her clitoris.

Having something in there for the wife's vaginal walls to grasp as she approaches orgasm may feel good. Some women say that as they reach sexual plateau they sense something missing. The wife may crave being filled. Other women don't feel much at all.

Using fingers as a surrogate penis works best if the husband is using two hands—one to stimulate his wife's clitoris and the other hand to stimulate her vagina. Continual stimulation of her clitoris or the area nearby will probably be required.

While that is happening, the husband's fingers can do a motion no penis can do. He can insert a finger or fingers in his wife's vagina with his palm up (assuming she is on her back). Instead of going in and out, he can curl his fingers. It's a "come here" motion. There is a ridged or rough spot on the upper wall of the engorged vagina. That's the spot to massage with the come-here motion.

The ridged spot on the upper wall of the vagina is something sometimes called the G spot (named for the German gynecologist Ernst Gräfenberg). The G spot is an area on the upper vaginal wall that may enjoy stimulation as a woman approaches orgasm. When the spot is pressed too early, she may feel a sudden need to urinate. That's the right spot just the wrong time. The G spot may be near parts of the interior clitoral structure where the clitoral body, *crura*, and vestibular bulbs all meet. Stimulating this part of the vagina may feel better to her than an in-and-out motion. Note that not all women perceive a G spot.

We've talked about how the wife will most likely need to focus her mental energy on her preferred sexual scene to progress. This doesn't mean she needs to be physically passive. Some women like to take an active role. She may enjoy grinding or rubbing her vulva against her husband's thigh or knee. She may enjoy touching her own erogenous zones to increase her pleasure. She may experiment to see how physically active she likes to be.

The husband should keep the stimulation steady all the way to his wife's orgasm. "Don't stop" means "don't stop"—*not* "faster and harder." "Don't stop" means "keep doing *exactly* that."

I had no idea about my clitoris!!! I mean, I knew it was there but the thought of getting pleasure from it.... Didn't happen for another ten years.

—Latter-day Saint wife, married at 23

I wish that I had known it takes women more than just penis-in-vagina sex to orgasm.

—Latter-day Saint husband, married at 23

Lips on Lips

For many women, the surefire, never miss, Old Faithful route to orgasm is oral sex. For some women, receiving oral sex (also called cunnilingus or going down) is the *only* way they orgasm. When a woman is ready—either because she is getting chafed by her husband's hand or because she just wants it—it can be time to bring his mouth to the field.

The tongue is magic. If you lick your own palm, you can feel your tongue go from soft to hard, from gentle to darting. A husband's tongue may end up being his wife's main sexual stimulator over the years. Nearly all women (95%) enjoy receiving oral sex. If a wife doesn't like receiving oral sex the first time, we suggest she try it a few more times before giving up on the experience. Some tastes are acquired. Husbands may not know how to give oral sex well at first.

Cunnilingus is not a start-from-zero experience. She will have to be ready for his tongue. This means he will start with about twenty minutes of non-genital touching before he begins oral sex.

Teasing a wife can increase her arousal. Her

husband can spiral in, kissing her inner thighs and *mons* as he works his way slowly to her vulva. If she is wearing garments or lingerie, he can breathe through the fabric, which can feel nice. Once she is naked, he can kiss her outer labia and finally start the serious stuff.

The man will have to get in there. He will have to be close, with his face pressed against his wife's skin. He will make the experience more pleasurable for her if he tells her he enjoys doing it. This may seem like a little thing, but it can be a big deal. She may be embarrassed to have him in such an intimate position. She may not be comfortable with how her vulva looks or smells. This is a sex parking brake issue. His enthusiasm helps release her sex parking brake so she can lose herself in the moment.

He will smell his wife. Vaginal secretions contain at least 2,100 odiferous compounds. Those compounds give her a unique scent. Some wives are embarrassed about it. She might even avoid receiving oral sex altogether if she worries her husband dislikes her smell. A thoughtful husband will reassure his wife that he enjoys everything about her vulva, including her odor. It's true that some new odors can be off-putting the first time we smell them. He should expect that over time he will become accustomed to his wife's scent. He will learn to associate her scent with sex. Like Pavlov's dogs and the dinner bell, he may look forward to her special smell.

As the wife lies on her back, she can position her legs the way she likes. Each way will give her different sensations. She can keep her legs straight and together for focused clitoral stimulation. The best access for him to reach her vulva will be with her legs bent and spread. She can put her feet on the bed, rest them on his back, or brace them on his shoulders. She can roll on her side and grip his head with her thighs. This may be a restful position for both husband and wife.

It can be helpful (less distracting) if he has a towel handy to mop up saliva or even to position under her buttocks from the get-go.

The husband should probably use a soft, fat tongue. Women complain that men tend to lick with a tongue that is too pointed. The couple can experiment to see what tongue firmness feels best to her.

The best motion for her will probably be on or near her clitoris and up-down or endless upstrokes. She may also like left-right or circular. Important: Making the tongue into a mini-penis and giving an in-out motion in the vagina does not do it for most women. Men tend to go for the in-out motion (what they would like) and not the clitoral stimulation she needs. The clitoris is where it's at.

Fun fact: When he is facing her, left and right are reversed. Following directions during cunnilingus is a constant test of his orientation skills. "Left. Left. LEFT. I SAID LEFT!" Good times.

He should get into a rhythm and keep to it. Steady stimulation is the name of the game. Usually. A few women are desensitized by repetitive motion and will need their man to mix things up. It will help him if she gives directions.

If the wife doesn't want to talk, she can move his head to the correct spot.

The husband's hands may do other things his wife enjoys while he licks:

- ❧ Caress her breasts.
- ❧ Rub her inner labia.
- ❧ Stimulate her vaginal opening.
- ❧ Insert a finger or fingers into her vagina to give her something to grip.
- ❧ Rub the ridged patch on the upper wall of her vagina (G spot).
- ❧ Reach around her thigh and massage her *mons*. He can pull her *mons* up toward her navel. This may feel nice to her. He can pull her *mons* up, pause, then let it down, and repeat.
- ❧ Touch her perineum (the area between her vagina and her anus) or her anus.
- ❧ Combine touches with each hand caressing a different place.

If a wife pushes her husband's head in an unexpected direction, he shouldn't resist. She may be placing him on a good spot or away from a spot that has become too sensitive. She's the expert.

If he is getting his circulation cut off or can't breathe, he can reposition himself. Telling her that she's tiring him or that he is starting to get cramped can distract her from her enjoyment. He has neither to suffer in silence nor to start to hint it's taking too long (it's *never* too long). He should just get in a more comfortable position and carry on.

The husband should keep going for as long as his wife wants. Expect twenty minutes or longer of direct clitoral stimulation. If she says "keep going," she doesn't mean "do it faster." Most women report they need consistency for their excitement to build. Finding the right rhythm and motion may help her build sexual tension and push her up over the edge of Mt. Climax.

As the wife is in each stage of her sexual response cycle—excitement, plateau, climax, and resolution with its post-orgasmic contentment (afterglow)—which parts of her body she wants touched and how may change. For example, she may want her face and arms caressed while her excitement builds but then have her husband focus his touch on her *mons* once she reaches her plateau and stay there through resolution. At plateau, she may feel her nipples want to be touched but then avoided altogether as she climaxes. She may like her buttocks to be grasped as she tenses for orgasm—or whatever.

A husband should build a mental blueprint of his wife's unique preferences as the couple banks a lifetime of shared sexual experience.

As a woman gets more familiar with her orgasmic pattern, she may be confident enough to edge close to orgasm, signal her husband to back off for a bit, then let herself approach orgasm again. Approaching then backing away from orgasm is called edging. Edging prolongs pleasure at its height. Most people edge. The risk to edging is that she may lose the edge, so to speak, and find herself unable to regain her orgasmic build.

What a husband does immediately after his wife orgasms and starts to enter her sexual resolution can change a typical climax into a more pleasurable experience for her. What he does or doesn't do during her later orgasmic spasms can make a difference in how long her orgasm will last. He will have to pay close attention to when it's not enough or too much.

To extend his wife's climax, a husband should not stop completely after she may seem to be finished. He will probably have to lighten up the motion for a bit to avoid overstimulation. He should pay close attention and notice if and when her sexual tension is rebuilding and try to amp it up at those times. This is different from the previous need to keep to a very consistent rhythm. She may be returned to the orgasmic state in waves, depending on what movements allow her to regain her sexual tension. Each orgasmic spasm becomes a mini-build. The motion may need to start lighter and less direct. If her tension builds, he may be able to move the motion more directly on or near the *glans* of her clitoris. If she should have another orgasmic spasm, he can then back off and try to let the tension build again.

For example, this could be a light licking that starts below the wife's clitoris then works its way slowly up to just hitting her clitoral *glans*. If she does not seem to tense up, her husband may return to licking lightly below her clitoris and then try again in a few seconds. If she does tense up as his tongue approaches her clitoris, he can reach the *glans* then stay on it until the tension subsides or she has another orgasmic spasm.

The technique of extending a wife's orgasm blends smoothly into the territory of multiple orgasms. Some women may fluctuate between plateau and orgasm. One in seven women self-report having multiple orgasms at least some of the time, where a full orgasm restarts after a brief refractory period.

A thoughtful husband may gently stimulate his wife after orgasm to see if she starts to get sexually tense again or instead says she is done.

When she says it's done, it's not quite done. Cuddle. Cuddling following orgasm is *important*. Those who cuddle after orgasm report higher satisfaction with their relationships and with sex. This is especially true of women and young parents.

Best part of married sex? Ha ha, the orgasms from oral! And of course the connection and fulfillment it brings.

—Latter-day Saint wife, married at 24

I love to please my wife in this way. She's does not enjoy giving, but loves to receive, so I do not ask any more and I'm okay with that.

—Latter-day Saint husband, married at 24

The Iron Rod

The first time a woman sees an erect penis, it may not be quite what she had expected. This is especially true if she changed diapers and assumed the tiny thing her little brother had would be the same as her husband's just...bigger. Nope. The mature penis is kind of amazing. In a few heartbeats it can werewolf-transform from a mild-mannered worm to a pulsing, veiny, sticking out, what-is-that-THING? A sex-ready penis bears only passing resemblance to the nib she may remember.

Unlike a vulva, where everything has to be just so for things to work, a penis is a high-tolerance tool. Even "bad" penis stimulation can end well for him. If he can achieve an erection and receives stimulation, his orgasm is almost guaranteed. It's not about where you end up so much as about how you get there.

The main ways a wife can stimulate her husband's penis are hand, mouth, vibrator, and vagina. Each will feel different to him. Some he will prefer more than others. All will (usually) work.

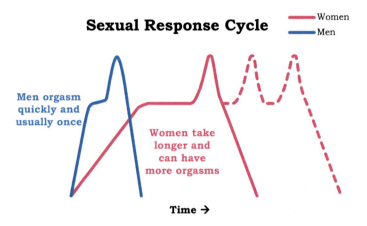

An orgasm by hand can be his quickest and most intense but not necessarily the most satisfying to him. Oral sex can be exciting or overstimulating, depending on how she uses her mouth and how his penis reacts. A vibrator gives him a unique feeling. Her vagina will give him a silky sensation unlike any other and may be the most emotionally satisfying.

Intercourse with a condom is a different feeling, where light sensations are dampened but big movements can be felt. Sex with a condom is like music with the treble turned off. It's still music, but it's not the same.

A husband can rub his penis against practically any part of his wife's body until he orgasms. Her armpit can work. Between her breasts can work if she presses them together around his penis. He can thrust between her closed thighs. Her anus can be tried if the couple wishes (use lots of lube; don't move bacteria from anus to places where bacteria shouldn't be, such as the vagina; move carefully so she is not hurt; and wash afterwards). The go-tos will probably be her hand, mouth, and vagina.

The husband probably knows exactly how he likes to be stimulated by hand. He may put his hand over his wife's to help guide her in the motions he likes. Working hand in hand may increase the couple's feeling of unity. If she lies down next to him, she can do it the way he likes using the hand he prefers. Left hands feel different from right hands on a penis. The motion will probably be *much* faster and more direct than she expects. All that delicate stuff she needs in order to get ready: He won't need it. An erection is all a man needs to be physically ready for intense genital stimulation if he wants it.

The husband will probably want the lights on and for his wife to be naked. The sight of her best parts will arouse him. Different body parts visually trigger different men. He can tell her what he wants to see. If she is to give her husband what he wants sexually, she will most likely be letting him stare at her nude body. This will not be a casual glance. He may stare at parts of her as though they are pieces of pie he's going to gobble up just as soon as he's examined every square inch. It's a sexual stare. She may feel uncomfortable, especially if she is self-conscious. We recommend the wife let her husband look. Looking at her body will enhance his arousal. In fact, he may need to look away so he doesn't orgasm sooner than he wants.

If the husband doesn't yet know what touch he likes or is too embarrassed to show his wife, a good first expectation is that she will be stroking the shaft of his penis rather than rubbing the tip. The tip of his penis may be too sensitive for direct stimulation. Or he may want her to rub the tip. Different men are different. There is a spot on his penis called the frenulum that is a common best spot for stimulation. The frenulum is found on the underside below the tip. She should look for a soft set of "accordion" folds of skin. Rubbing that spot will probably feel extra nice.

A wife may give her husband a "hand job" with a wet or dry palm. He may like it dry, in which case she will hold the skin of his shaft with moderate pressure and move that skin rhythmically up toward his tip and down towards his body. A dry hand doesn't slip along the skin. Instead, his soft skin will move with her hand while his hard shaft stays relatively still.

He may like it wet, in which case her lubricated hand will slip over his penis and up and down his shaft. Water doesn't work well for this. A commercial lubricant may be used. If she has enough vaginal lubrication to share, she can use that. Saliva works temporarily but must be reapplied because it dries quickly.

Up and down isn't the only possible motion, especially with a lubricated penis. She can experiment with two hands and different movements, including rubbing or twisting motions.

Wet or dry, he will probably want her to settle

into a rhythm. He can coach her on the range of motion he prefers. It may feel best to him if the inside of her pointer and middle fingers contact his frenulum as she stimulates him. He can tell her when he wants it faster or slower.

If the husband asks his wife to slow down or stop, she should do that. It can be exciting for him to edge close to orgasm then back away. He can tell her when to speed back up.

The wife may add to her husband's sensations by caressing his other erogenous zones with a free hand, her lips, her tongue, or her body. He may like his neck or face stroked. He may like his earlobes or nipples touched. He may like to kiss. He may like her to brush against him with her breasts or vulva, or he may want to touch her. He may like to touch himself in some places while she touches him in others. The couple can experiment to see what touches he enjoys.

She may be wondering what, if anything, to do with her husband's scrotum, the sac of skin containing his testicles. The scrotum is a high-risk zone. Bumping or squeezing his testicles too hard will hurt. Even a mild tap can ache for some men. That's the risk. The reward is the erotic value to exploring his scrotum *gently*. His scrotum is skin similar to her outer labia. Fondling or cupping his scrotum may be exciting for him. If she is using lubrication, she can close her fingers in an a-okay sign around the base of his scrotum to pull back his skin from his penis to make the skin taut. Or he may want her to stay far away from his testicles. He won't be shy to give feedback on this one.

There is a technique to try if the husband finds rubbing his penis tip to be overstimulating. As he approaches orgasm, his wife can hold the palm of her free hand just in front of his penis tip so he can thrust into her palm. Since he controls the motion, he can keep himself from being overstimulated. This will allow him to get a bit more sensation at the end than he otherwise would be able to tolerate.

A few minutes after a wife begins stimulating her husband's penis in a way that he likes, he will tense up. Most but not all men prefer harder and faster stimulation as orgasm approaches. Some men prefer a very hard, very fast motion at climax. Other men want a more constant speed. Then he will orgasm and ejaculate.

His orgasm feels like hers: fantastic. His blood pressure will spike. Muscles all over his body will clench. His face may look as if he's in pain. His toes, like hers, may curl up except the sticking-straight-out big toe. He may moan or grunt. His brain may go into a dream state. Shortly after his orgasm begins, semen will pump out of the hole at the tip of his penis. His orgasm will probably be shorter than hers—about five to fifteen seconds. His orgasmic contractions may come with clockwork regularity of 0.8 seconds or be irregular. Endorphins will flood his blood as his brain rewards him for sex and bonds him to her.

Ejaculation may be interesting and fun. A wife may have a sense of accomplishment. "I did that!" Or she may find ejaculate to be repellant. She may want to modify her natural reaction if it's negative so his experience is one of love. Her husband may feel premarital guilt about orgasm by hand, so expressing love is one way to have him turn an experience that he may view from his past as shameful to one that is a deep expression of acceptance. She may be able to help him recapture his sense of sexual well-being.

One thing a wife will need experience to know is when to stop. The penis becomes more sensitive during and after orgasm. Continued touching at a slower rate can be enjoyable for a man. One thing he will almost certainly want is for her to wait until he says to let go. He may seem to be done and just lying there, but he may have one final wave building. This wave may stop if her hand is removed. The feeling of a penis being held after orgasm is pleasant and feels safe. It's probably best not to let go until he says it's time.

He may fall asleep for a bit after orgasm. This is normal. It's entirely physical. A post-orgasmic man experiences a drop in blood pressure and a flood of hormones that may make him conk out. He still cares. It just means he had a good time. He's likely to wake up in a few minutes.

After orgasm, the couple should cuddle to bond. His penis will shrink and return to its resting state.

I wish I had known what a penis looked like, both soft and erect.

—*Latter-day Saint wife, married at 22*

I wish I had known how to give him a good hand job with lotion twenty years earlier in our marriage. This would have made him so much happier on all the occasions when I said, "Not tonight."

—*Latter-day Saint wife, married at 22*

Kissing It

A wife's most important oral-sex technique is enthusiasm. Oral sex may be done well with any technique so long as a husband sees his wife is enthusiastic to do it. Receiving oral sex can be affirming to him—physical proof his wife cherishes his sexual self. Words men use to describe how they feel receiving oral sex are *wanted*, *respected*, and *accepted*. Oral sex scratches a psychological itch in many men.

Nearly all men (97%) enjoy receiving oral sex, also called fellatio or a blow job. Although this act is often called a blow job, there may not be actual blowing involved. There are two main ways a wife can give her husband oral stimulation. She can use her lips and tongue to provide the motion, or she can let him thrust.

There are many spots to lick and ways to lick them. Different licks on different spots feel different. A wife can ice-cream-cone lick or can flick her tongue. She can use a soft or hard tongue. She can kiss. She can suck. She can lick along the shaft or focus on the tip. He may enjoy if she gives extra attention to his frenulum, which is on the underside of his penis near where the head meets the shaft. He should tell her if it's feeling good. A wife is not a mind reader.

While a wife uses her mouth to pleasure her husband, she may use her hands to stimulate other parts he likes to have touched. These may include the shaft of his penis, especially if she uses lubrication. She may run her hands across his skin, run her fingers through his pubic hair, stroke his thighs, grab his buttocks, caress his testicles (carefully), or massage his perineum. Different men prefer different touches.

A more intercourse-like approach may be preferred where the wife may let her husband thrust against her lips and tongue. She can bob her head while he holds still, or she may hold her head still while he moves against her lips and tongue. If he likes to thrust, he can control the timing and rhythm the way he prefers.

A downside of thrusting during oral sex is that the husband might cause his wife to gag. This is especially true if he tries to grab her by the back of her head and mash himself into her face (he shouldn't do this unless the couple is into this and she is prepared). A wife shouldn't have to gag for him to have a good time. Most women do not enjoy the sensation of a penis in the back of the throat. She can limit how far he can push his penis in her mouth by gripping the base of his shaft. This blocks how deeply he can thrust.

As the husband reaches his point of no return, his wife has to decide what she wants to do to finish him off. Leaving him to orgasm without any stimulation at the end may be sexually unsatisfying to him. She may use her hand to stimulate him as he completes his orgasm, or she can accept his ejaculate in her mouth.

If a wife allows her husband to ejaculate in her mouth, there is the question of what to do with the semen. She can swallow it. It's sterile, natural, and safe. Semen in her mouth won't make her pregnant. If she doesn't want to swallow, she can keep tissue paper handy where she can spit. She can also hang out around his penis for a minute with her mouth open and let gravity do its work.

Note that not all men can or want to orgasm from fellatio. A husband may prefer to start with oral sex then orgasm through other forms of stimulation. Fellatio can be foreplay.

A shower is a good venue for fellatio. A wife may prefer her husband have freshly washed genitals. The water can provide some lubrication for her hands. Cleaning up semen in the shower is a snap. She can rinse her mouth easily afterwards if she wishes.

There is an oral-sex option for letting the husband thrust without some of the downsides. His penis will not be in her mouth with this technique. He will lie on his back. She may cup his shaft with a hand so it is between his penis and his pubic hair. She will push "duck lips" or "kissy lips" against his frenulum. She can move up and down the penis shaft or let him thrust against her lips. Since his penis is not in her mouth, he can thrust as hard and as far as he likes. He can even push her head against his penis to increase the intensity.

For a husband, receiving oral sex is an act of faith. He will be vulnerable. A wife will have her teeth around her husband's most precious part. He must trust her. She affirms that trust when she chooses to give him pleasure.

Fellatio can be a deeply intimate act. Both husband and wife must be present in the moment. There is nowhere to hide. Her thoughts play across her face. His emotions are exposed to all her senses. There is a symbolism to a wife accepting her husband's organ of sex into her organ of speech. The act is a unique discourse of love.

Oral sex is amazing if done right.
—Latter-day Saint husband, married at 20

My husband loves when I perform oral sex on him. I actually enjoy giving him that pleasure because of how much he enjoys it. It's a selfless sexual act I give to him because it makes him happy.
—Latter-day Saint wife, married at 22

Positions

Most women cannot orgasm with penis in vagina (intercourse) alone. It's perfectly normal not to be able to do it the way the movies show. You know the scene—both woman and man gasp at the same time with no hands down there to stimulate the clitoris. It doesn't work like that in real life.

Intercourse is a male-centric mode of sex. The husband likely orgasms. The wife likely doesn't. This is not to say women dislike intercourse. Both men and women find intercourse to be enjoyable in its own right even if it doesn't end in orgasm. Intercourse is erotic, and the couple can bond over the closeness of the act. There is also the excitement of a potential pregnancy if that's desired.

A couple cannot start intercourse from zero and expect it to end in orgasm for them both. The timing seldom works. A husband can complete his entire arousal cycle in minutes or seconds, while his wife is nowhere near plateau—let alone orgasm.

For women who do orgasm in intercourse, they

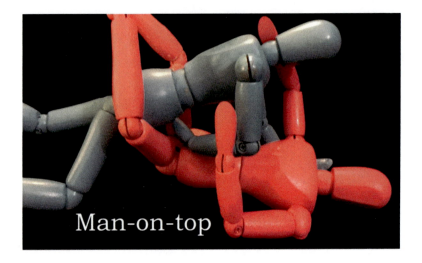

Man-on-top

already most often have been stimulated to the edge with foreplay before a penis gets into the act. This means hand, mouth, or vibrator stimulation with the wife telling her husband when it's time to switch to his penis...plus. Her clitoris will need extra stimulation.

Assuming the couple is ready for intercourse, there is the matter of position. Sex manuals are all about position. So many positions. So many names. So little that's meaningful.

All couples find sex positions that are their favorites. Experiment. Some positions feel spot on for a wife and less so for a husband. Vice versa for others. Some feel more loving. Some feel more erotic. Some feel sweet. Some feel primal. Different positions suit different moods.

Different positions may provide the couple sexual novelty. Human brains seek sexual novelty

Woman-on-top

and get an extra chemical boost from the unfamiliar during sex. Varying positions can help provide an additional erotic thrill without going outside the marriage to get that thrill. Novel positions can help keep sex exciting.

Nonetheless, couples tend to return to preferred positions over and over with minor variations. These are the most common positions for intercourse.

Man-on-top (missionary position): In the man-on-top position, the husband does more physical work. He rests his weight on his hands or elbows so he doesn't crush his wife. Variations mostly involve where she puts her legs—with her ankles on his shoulders, entwined around him, or braced on the surface of the bed. Both legs can be at the same angle, or one can be up and the other down. Other variations involve the man kneeling,

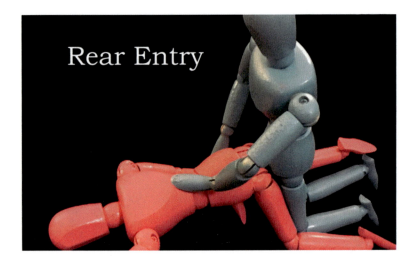

Rear Entry

squatting, or standing off the side of the bed. A pillow placed under her buttocks can change the angle and make things feel different.

Woman-on-top: In the woman-on-top position, the couple faces each other (cowgirl) or the wife turns around and faces her husband's feet (reverse cowgirl). He will be able to see and touch his wife's breasts or buttocks, depending on which way she faces. The woman works harder in this position and has more control over the motions. Some women are able to orgasm in intercourse only when they are on top and can control the angle and rhythm.

Rear entry: In rear entry, the husband enters his wife's vagina from behind. She may be on her hands and knees (sometimes called doggy style or table top). This position can be vigorous and deep. Women report unique sensations from rear entry.

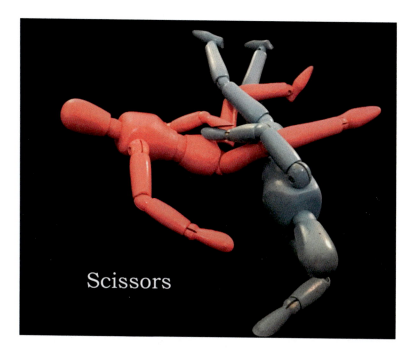

Scissors

Husbands may enjoy a good view of their wife's buttocks.

Spooning is a variation on rear entry with the spouses lying on their sides. Spooning tends to be more gentle, and his penis is less deep.

Scissors: The scissors position is physically easy for both spouses. The wife lies on her back as though ready for man-on-top. Her husband lies on his side at ninety degrees to his wife. He scissors her far thigh (top and bottom) with both his thighs. Her near leg rests on top of her husband's hip. If he is on his wife's right side, his feet will be toward the left side of the bed. The leg order from floor to ceiling is man left, woman left, man right, woman right. It's like Twister but better.

Scissors may work better than other positions for those with physical challenges or for pregnant couples. A couple can go to sleep in the scissors position after intercourse. Scissors is comfy.

These positions do not comprise an exhaustive list. These are just ideas a couple can use as starting points for their own experimentation.

Three notes on the wife's pleasure: First, for her to climax during intercourse, her clitoris will most likely be stimulated directly with a vibrator or a hand—either hers or her husband's. Some positions provide easier access to the clitoris for one or both spouses. Second, while he may prefer an in-and-out motion, a grinding motion of his pubic bone on hers may give her more sensation than his penis ever could. Third—and this cannot be stated too often—she may find intercourse to be enjoyable even if it's not a reliable way for her to orgasm.

Missionary style is not the only position to have sex in.

—Latter-day Saint wife, married at 25

I enjoy variations of spooning from the side, me (the woman) on top either straddling or reverse cowgirl position. "Missionary" is my least favorite as I don't feel my husband as well in that position.

—Latter-day Saint wife, married at 22

The First Time

When men and women describe their first intercourse, we hear two *very* different stories. One might wonder if they were even in the same bedroom.

As a rule, a man describes his first time as pretty good. It might not have been the best sex. Maybe it was a bit awkward. It was probably over too fast. But he climaxed, and things pretty much worked out. For him.

That's not what women say. The one word that sums up what most women say about first intercourse is *disappointing.*

Here are the things couples say went wrong for them. The man didn't know (or didn't care) to give the woman foreplay. She was in pain when he inserted because she wasn't aroused enough to have a penis in her vagina comfortably. First intercourse was over too quickly for her. She may have bled.

With expectations appropriately low, let's talk about what a couple can do to make first intercourse better for the woman. The good news is that typical first-intercourse problems can be solved with awareness and some prep work. There is no reason first intercourse has to be disappointing. The first time can be enjoyable for all.

The very first time a woman has intercourse, she may have an intact hymen. This is a tag of vaginal flesh that may get a small tear the first time a penis is in there. Not every woman has a hymen that will tear, even if she is a virgin. Tampons stretch out the hymen. Hymens tear normally in the course of life. If the wife is anxious about it, she may ask her gynecologist before the wedding to examine her and decide if a small procedure will make it so there is less stress for her the first time she has intercourse.

The most likely cause of painful first intercourse is insufficient foreplay. Even first penetration may be enjoyable for a woman if she is sufficiently aroused. First-intercourse foreplay may be done effectively with oral sex. Even if she doesn't orgasm, the foreplay will help prepare her vagina. Saliva will also help hydrate the region. Sliding a penis into a wet vagina is approximately an infinity times less painful than shoving it into a dry one.

If a wife has an orgasm before intercourse, the physical changes that prepare her vagina for insertion will be complete. She will be more lubricated. Her vaginal opening will be wider, and her vagina will be longer. Her genitals will be engorged with blood and ready for a thrusting penis.

Part of first-penetration pain may be

psychological. If the wife fears insertion, it's more likely to hurt. Some women are warned that sex will hurt, and anxiety can make it so. Sex is not supposed to hurt. Waiting until she actively wants the experience will make it more pleasurable for her.

The husband or wife can gently separate her labia before intercourse. If she has pubic hair that's a bit tangled, separating the labia also will get the hair out of the way.

A couple shouldn't be afraid to use additional lubrication, especially the first time. "The wetter the better" is how many couples like it. It's wise to have some on hand. Water-based or silicone-based lubricants can change a couple's sex life from one of discomfort to one of slippery fun. Coconut oil may also be used but not with condoms. Different lubricants feel different. Some people are allergic to some ingredients. A couple may need to do some research and try several lubricants before finding a good match.

This is going to sound dumb if you haven't tried, but this is serious. You have to find the right spot. The penis goes into the vagina. Not just randomly in the folds of her labia. Not accidentally into her anus. Not, as happened to a poor wife described in a medical journal, into her urethra. The husband can look down there to see what's going on. The opening of the vagina may be lower than he expects.

Can it be that difficult to find the right spot? Yes, yes, it can. Our genitals are very sensitive, but the sensitivity is not like the sensitivity of a fingertip. We can read Braille with our fingers. We can read Braille with our lips. We can't read Braille, even if we were so inclined, with our genitals. We don't have the right kind of nerves. So don't try this at home, boys. "Down there" is not mentally tethered in space the same way as other parts of our bodies. It can be difficult to know just where, exactly, our genitals are. Inserting a penis into a vagina can be surprisingly challenging if we don't keep our eye on the ball, so to speak. You may not be able to tell where you both are without feeling around with a hand or looking. If you have to do it by feel, one of you should probably use a hand to guide the tip home. Putting in a penis may best be left to the wife, especially if she uses tampons. She knows right where it goes.

By the way, we never do grow the right nerves to pinpoint our own genitals in space, so getting the penis in the right spot may be a source of goofy amusement for the rest of you and your spouse's mortality together. Enjoy!

A husband should push his penis in slowly the first time. Better yet, the wife can be in the woman-on-top position and control the speed of entry. She may have some light bleeding during first intercourse even if they move slowly and she is well lubricated. There may be some stretching involved, especially if he has a large penis.

What is *not* normal is for the vagina to be impossible to enter. If a couple finds that the vagina seems to seal shut, it's important not to force things. Stop. Relax. The wife may be experiencing an uncommon condition called vaginismus. Her body will have to learn insertion isn't painful, so don't make things worse. The couple can do oral or hand sex for now. Vaginismus is rare, but if it happens to you, *don't force things*. She can call her gynecologist in the morning. They've heard it many times before. Embrace that your marriage's sexual awakening will be in stages not compressed into one night. That's enjoyable, too! Read the "When to Call a Professional" chapter for more information.

One spouse may be much more sexually experienced than the other. Past sexual experience brings both plusses and minuses to the marriage bed. On the plus side, a sexually experienced spouse may bring know-how and realistic expectations to the wedding night. This can be an asset. For example, if the wife already knows how she needs to be touched to reach orgasm, the couple can start their sexual journey together headed the right way for her. If the husband knows from experience about foreplay and how to insert without causing pain, the wife need not be traumatized by first intercourse.

One liability of prior sexual experience is that the less experienced spouse may feel insecure. The insecurity may tempt that spouse to shame the more experienced spouse. "Did you learn this from...?" is an all-to-human question but can be a wedge Satan *will* try drive right into the heartwood of a marriage. Be aware. The less experienced spouse may need reassurance that he or she is attractive, sexually fulfilling, "the chosen one." The more experienced spouse may need acceptance from the less experienced spouse to feel that sins are forgiven and that the past does not haunt the marriage.

Once intercourse has started, a virgin man will usually have an orgasm quickly. His wife will be unlikely to orgasm from the much-too-quick friction of a much-too-inexperienced husband. They should work together to make sure she gets the stimulation she'd like another way.

After intercourse, semen does not stay put. Some of it drains out. If this bothers you, you can have tissues or a towel handy.

This is a milestone for you both. You've had Sex with a Capital "S." It's your first time together or first time ever, which is a huge step in anyone's life. There are many emotions you feel the first time. First intercourse can be a wonderful bonding experience. The sense of love and unity may surprise you both.

I was so naïve. I didn't understand how big a man's penis was when fully erect. I didn't know how MESSY sex would be or how awkward. I honestly knew it wouldn't be like a movie but was still somehow expecting it to be amazing. I remember thinking, "That's it? That's what all the fuss has been about?"

—Latter-day Saint wife, married at 20

It gets better. We both knew it would but those first few weeks were frustrating as we figured things out.

—Latter-day Saint husband, married at 33

Temple Wedding, Honeymoon in Hell

We surveyed Latter-day Saints on the Eternal Marriage Bed Facebook group about what surprised them on their wedding nights. What happened that they weren't expecting about the sexual experience? What did they wish they had known at the time? Ninety-five couples responded. Most of these couples tell a story of newlyweds who entered marriage knowing too little to make the wedding night joyful.

The bad news is that the unprepared Latter-day Saint couple may be blindsided by painful intercourse and a lack of a pleasurable sexual experience for the wife. The good news is that a prepared couple may minimize or even avoid completely these unpleasant wedding-night surprises.

And ye shall know the truth, and the truth shall make you free.

—John 8:32

Read what these couples said about their wedding night. Think how much better the first fully sexual experience of these Latter-day Saints' marriages might have been. Think about what you have learned so far and how you might prepare as a couple so your own wedding night can be enjoyable to you both. Knowing about foreplay, lubrication, and patience all can help.

I knew almost nothing about foreplay. I wish I knew more about sex so it could have been something fun, happy and amazing instead.
—Latter-day Saint wife, married at 23

I knew penetration may be difficult, but I didn't understand how difficult, nor was I prepared to see blood. I didn't realize how much lube would have helped.
—Latter-day Saint husband, married at 23

We had no lubricant and literally couldn't penetrate because of it.
—Latter-day Saint wife, married at 18

I had no idea sex would be painful for my wife.
—Latter-day Saint husband, married at 23

The wedding night was scary and painful because I didn't know how great it could be.
—Latter-day Saint wife, married at 22

We were shy and awkward. I didn't orgasm, and his just sort of happened. The previous sexual tension got overshadowed by the newness and nervousness of finally doing it. We woke up a few hours later and tried again because I was upset about how the first one was so anticlimactic. Still no orgasm for me, but better.
—Latter-day Saint wife, married at 21

I was terrified to be intimate. I was scared because all of my family and friends knew what we were doing. I was not even a virgin, and neither was he, but the thought that my family knew what I was

doing was very scary, and caused us to not have sex that night. It actually caused me to have intimacy problems for the first few years of my marriage.
—Latter-day Saint wife, married at 23

I thought something was wrong with me.
—Latter-day Saint husband, married at 21

I didn't expect the first time to be over so fast.
—Latter-day Saint husband, married at 23

Many couples wished they had received a better sex education prior to the wedding night. Common "I wish I had known" themes centered on female sexual pleasure and penetrative sex.

I wish I had known manual stimulation was important for women to enjoy sex...critical for a woman to orgasm. It took more than a year.
—Latter-day Saint husband, married at 22

I wish I knew more about my clitoris and its role in sex. I had Sex ed growing up (don't remember having the talk with my parents), and I didn't know about my clitoris or even where it was before getting married. All I ever heard of was the "G spot."
—Latter-day Saint wife, married at 24

I wish I'd known how a woman truly experiences sex and about the female orgasm. We could have avoided so many issues.
—Latter-day Saint husband, married at 22

I wish I had known to use lots of lube, and foreplay before. Also that sex most likely won't end in orgasm (female) and that's okay!
—Latter-day Saint wife, married at 24

I wish I had known it could be enjoyable for women and that I could orgasm. I always heard women in

the church complain about having sex with their husbands and saying it only feels good for the guy. I grew up only hearing negative things about sex, and I was absolutely terrified of it.
—Latter-day Saint wife, married at 22

I wish I would have known about lube and foreplay. I wish I would have known about orgasms, and I wish I would have known my own anatomy better.
—Latter-day Saint wife, married at 22

I had no idea females were capable of having pleasure. I had no idea that it was OK. I just knew how babies were made.
—Latter-day Saint wife, married at 20

I mean, any sex education would have been helpful. Specifically, I wish we had both known more about the process of having penetrative sex for the first time. I tried to be gentle and slow, and I only went as far and as fast as she told me to go, but it was still bloody and painful for her, and I felt like a monster. Even just knowing about how to use lube would have been helpful. Also, I wish we both had known more about female orgasm, foreplay, and how to please each other separately—that sex isn't just penis-in-vagina.
—Latter-day Saint husband, married at 23

I wish I had known pretty much everything since neither of us knew anything.
—Latter-day Saint husband, married at 21

In contrast, some couples said they were prepared for the wedding night. Based on their reported wedding-night histories, first sex seemed to go better for the prepared. Even those who didn't have the best physical experience felt more at ease. They knew that sex would get better after the first time.

I knew plenty about sex from books (pre-Internet era).
—*Latter-day Saint wife, married at 22*

I had read a lot and I came from a very open family so I felt adequately prepared, to be honest.
—*Latter-day Saint husband, married at 33*

Luckily my husband knew that sex was supposed to feel good for the women as well as the man so things got better.
—*Latter-day Saint wife, married at 22*

I wasn't expecting how big my hubby's member was inside me. Otherwise, I felt confident about everything.
—*Latter-day Saint wife, married at 21*

I honestly don't feel like there were many surprises.
—*Latter-day Saint wife, married at 21*

There wasn't really anything I was unaware of. Actually, it was a lot easier than I thought it would be.
—*Latter-day Saint wife, married at 22*

First-time sex can be a comedy of errors. A good attitude seemed to help some couples through missteps. Remember that everyone makes mistakes. Even wedding-night blunders can be a bonding experience and strengthen a marriage if the couple has a good attitude.

We had a wonderful mistake/miscommunication that led me to live by the motto "never leave her wanting." Others have coined it "she comes first."
—*Latter-day Saint husband, married at 24*

I didn't know that the birth control pills I was on would suppress my natural lubrication. It took us

several days of awkward tries before we achieved coitus. The good thing is, we were open in our communication as we worked through the awkwardness.
—Latter-day Saint wife, married at 22

Fortunately, I knew I didn't have to have a good time and also that we would figure it out.
—Latter-day Saint wife, married at 21

I knew that the penis went in the vagina, but I didn't know much about the vagina. I was confused that it didn't just "go in." Years later we laugh about it. "That's not it! That's not it either."
—Latter-day Saint husband, married at 24

Reading these accounts, a pattern emerges. On many Latter-day Saint couples' wedding nights, what the husband wanted and was ready for—intercourse—was usually what happened. He may have been familiar with his own sexual response and was ready for the next sexual progression. He didn't know female anatomy, the ways to pleasure a woman, or the time a woman needs to be touched before she is ready for intercourse.

What the wife might have been ready for wasn't part of any plan. She may not have learned what touches her body would find arousing. She might not even have had a clear idea of her own anatomy. She didn't know to ask for the foreplay she needed. She was unprepared in body and mind for intercourse.

The outcome was predictable in hindsight. The couple had intercourse before the wife was ready. She was in pain and had a bad experience. Tears were shed.

It didn't have to be this way. It doesn't have to be this way for you.

It seems to us the wedding night is too often based on the husband's plan with no input from the wife. You can build your marriage on a firmer foundation. Instead of his making all the decisions without input from her, you can make your first sexual experience as husband and wife a shared experience with shared decision-making. Talking about this may feel awkward. That awkwardness you will do well to push right through. It will be worth it. Whatever discomfort you may experience by planning the wedding night together can't be as bad as pain and tears.

A better honeymoon approach would be to talk about what you each want. The wife may want a drawn-out event with different sexual gifts to be opened each day. The wedding night will be lower pressure if the couple plans to be naked together and explore touching each other. Oral sex can be a gift the couple opens on a later night. Intercourse can be the last honeymoon gift to open—once she is *literally* begging for it.

The closer a couple gets to working as "one flesh"—planning together and deciding together before acting together—the more likely the couple will be together in their own Garden of Eden not a Honeymoon in Hell.

Some survey respondents chose to give advice to other Latter-day Saints preparing for the wedding night and beyond. We'll end this chapter with their words.

I would tell them to relax and be patient. Go slow!! Don't be embarrassed to talk to each other.
—Latter-day Saint wife, married at 22

Let HER decide when she's ready and don't force things.
—Latter-day Saint husband, married at 27

Don't focus on the end game. Just focus on enjoying each other's space and letting the progression of getting comfortable with each other happen naturally instead of trying to rush it and focusing on the inexperience and frustration.
—Latter-day Saint wife, married at 23

Foreplay, foreplay, foreplay.
—Latter-day Saint wife, married at 25

Read books from a Christian perspective or at least tasteful perspective and have a very open frank conversation—several of them—before so you are "eyes wide open."
—Latter-day Saint husband, married at 22

#1, Find her clitoris. #2, Sex is fun.
—Latter-day Saint wife, married at 23

Putting It All Together

If the wife can orgasm from intercourse—or if you both want to try to see if it can work for you—there are tricks that can help get her enough stimulation.

The highest hurdle standing between a woman and her orgasm is timing. Insertion must be timed so that she orgasms while her husband can still keep it up. Foreplay is a must. There is little chance she will orgasm if her genitals are unstimulated before intercourse.

We'll repeat that. Foreplay is a must. She will have to be well on her way to orgasm for intercourse to bring her the final piece of stimulation she needs.

Timing will also depend on how long he can maintain his erection. Some men can delay orgasm. Some men find intercourse to be so exciting that it's well-nigh impossible to hold back. Some men can sustain an erection after orgasm. Some cannot. A few men can orgasm twice or more in most sessions.

If the husband can sustain his erection after his orgasm, getting the wife enough stimulation will

Starting Intercourse Without Foreplay = Sad Wife

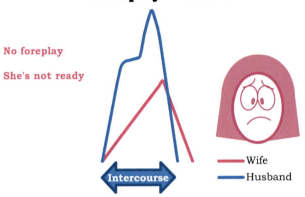

No foreplay

She's not ready

Intercourse

Wife
Husband

be easier. He can keep on keeping on until she has her turn.

Another option is a condom. Condoms reduce his sensation. This may be enough to get the timing right.

During intercourse, he can think of nonsexual, higher-brain things to delay his orgasm. The old standby is "think of baseball." These days we'd say "think about video games." Distancing the mind from sex is a bit of a killjoy. That's kind of the point.

Practice makes perfect. With practice, men can learn greater orgasmic control. See the start-stop and squeeze techniques in the "Misfires" chapter.

Getting the timing right is half the fun. The other half is getting the woman enough stimulation to get her to orgasm.

The sensitive *glans* of the clitoris is relatively far from the vagina. We hate to break it to you, men,

Clitoral Stimulation + Delaying Intercourse May Allow Her Orgasm

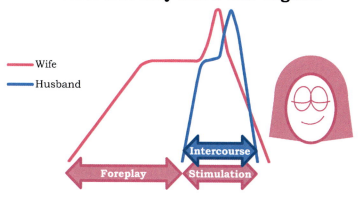

but your penis probably isn't what will get your wife off even if she enjoys intercourse. There are exceptions. One in five women can orgasm from intercourse alone. These women have something in common, and it's not the luck of the draw with his anatomy but with hers. The shorter the distance between her clitoris and her urethra, the more likely she is to orgasm during intercourse. If the wife has her clitoris positioned anatomically closer to where her husband's penis inserts, she is more likely to receive enough stimulation without hands.

The vast majority of women will need extra clitoral stimulation to have even a chance of reaching orgasm during intercourse. To get this added stimulation, the husband or wife can rub her clitoris.

A vibrator can be a reliable option. The couple may purchase a vibrator and apply that to her clitoris during intercourse. As of the writing of this book, both Wal-Mart and Target sell vibrators online (but Costco does not, which may come as a disappointment to many a Latter-day Saint consumer).

A husband may also increase his wife's clitoral stimulation by grinding with his pubic bone against hers rather than by thrusting.

Even if she doesn't absolutely require direct clitoral stimulation, just about all women find clitoral stimulation makes intercourse better.

A couple may try different intercourse positions to see which ones work best for the wife and still allow access to her clitoris. Some positions may allow her to control the timing or angle. Woman-on-top, where she has the most control, is a position that may work when others do not. The scissors position gives easy access to her clitoris with a hand or even the husband's upper thigh.

While the penis may not stimulate the clitoris well in most positions, if the penis is angled up to push against the woman's G-spot, this may give her deep clitoral sensation once she is fully aroused. Positions that more often allow for the G-spot to be stimulated include doggy style, spooning if the man has a large enough penis, woman-on-top with her facing him and sitting up fairly straight, and man-on-top with her feet resting on his shoulders.

One thing that comes up regularly in sex surveys is that the first thrust can be extra exciting to some women—sometimes the best part of intercourse. "It takes my breath away every time," said one. Some women report wanting one smooth stroke. Some want the first stroke to be teasing, with light pressure and then a slow push to full insertion. Some women say they enjoy the pop of the penis pushing past the outer third of the vagina. Some women enjoy it if man stops and lets her savor the sensation of having something inside her before he goes to town. A couple may experiment to find what first stroke the wife likes best.

It's important to recognize that some women feel no more from penis-in-vagina than from finger-in-mouth. Every woman is different. A wife can love her husband and enjoy intercourse but feel nearly nothing from his penis.

With or without an orgasm, couples tend to find intercourse to be loving, emotionally satisfying, and bonding. Intercourse is a physical *and* spiritual experience. Both men and women associate penis-in-vagina with a "coming home" feeling. Both women and men say intercourse can feel "just right," "safe," and "finally!"

For nearly the entire first year of marriage, sex was very unfulfilling for me. I cannot orgasm through penetration. At first I thought something was wrong with me. I mean, isn't that the ONLY way to orgasm? It wasn't until my husband went to the library to read books on the female orgasm that he learned there is a percentage of woman that orgasm through other methods and stimuli (i.e., fingering the clitoris). He has since learned and mastered those methods, and orgasms have always been achievable since. I'm so grateful he didn't give up and took the time to educate himself using books that explain in a non-pornographic way.
—Latter-day Saint wife, married at 22

It's rare to have a penile orgasm naturally. There needs to be a little help.
—Latter-day Saint husband, married at 23

Birth Control

Making babies is joyful. It's also a commandment. But when? When exactly to have children is a choice. Worrying about getting pregnant when you don't want it isn't joyful at all. Birth control can make unwanted pregnancy less likely.

> *The decision of how many children to have and when to have them is a private matter for the husband and wife.*
> — *LDS.org: "Birth Control"*

Having sex without contraception is very likely to end in pregnancy. About 85% of women get pregnant within a year of unprotected sex. The only surefire way not to have a baby is not to have any sperm enter the vagina. Even surgical sterilization, which the Church discourages, has a failure rate of about one pregnancy per hundred couples per year.

No single method of birth control works all of the time. One reason birth-control methods fail is human error. No birth-control method works if it isn't used right. You may have learned in health class how well different birth-control methods work in theory. Things are different in real life with real people making real decisions in the heat of the moment.

In real life, birth control is a case of the good, the not-so-bad, and the ugly.

The Good

Implants: Implants are small, plastic rods that are inserted under the skin of a woman's arm. Implants release birth-control hormones over time. Implants have a nearly perfect record in real life. Only 1 in 2,000 couples get pregnant. Couples report high satisfaction with implants.

IUDs: An IUD is a copper or plastic device that a doctor places in the uterus and leaves there for five, seven, or even ten years. IUDs block sperm and keep fertilized eggs from implanting. IUDs work more than 99% of the time. Couples report high satisfaction with IUDs. Family planners pick the IUD as their own birth-control method of choice. Fertility returns quickly after the doctor removes an IUD in most cases.

The Not-so-bad

The Pill, Patches, Shots, and Rings: These hormonal methods are very commonly used and have failure rates in real life of about 5%-10% each year.

The Minipill (progesterone only): The minipill has to be taken at the same time every day. The minipill has a 13% pregnancy rate in the first year, which is a bit worse than the regular pill (the regular pill also has estrogen and is a bit more forgiving in terms of dose timing).

The Ugly

Condoms: About one in five couples relying on condoms gets pregnant in a year. Condoms work great when they are used correctly, but in real life people don't use condoms as instructed. Condoms that are too large may slip off. (For *some reason* men pick out over-large condoms at the pharmacy aisle.) The penis has to be taken out of the vagina before the man's erection collapses, or semen may escape out the bottom of the condom. The condom has to be held to the base of the penis while the man pulls out, or the condom could slip off and make a bundle of joy in nine months.

Both men and women find sex with condoms to be less satisfying than skin-on-skin. It can be tempting to take a chance and not put the condom on "this once."

Some men pull off condoms on the sly, which is morally wrong everywhere and is criminal in some countries.

On the plus side, a man may be able to delay orgasm with a condom on.

Condoms earn a higher rating outside of marriage because condoms can prevent sexually transmitted infections. If the husband or wife has an incurable STI such as HIV or herpes, condoms will be necessary to minimize the chance of the infection spreading.

If you do choose to use condoms, actually read the directions. Condoms have to be put on and taken off properly. Confirm your lubrication is compatible with your condom. Oil-based lubricants eat away at latex and may cause a condom to break. Also, lubrication goes only on the outside of a condom.

Pulling Out: Pulling out doesn't work well at all in real life. The man is supposed to remove his penis from the vagina just before he ejaculates. The idea is simple and not much fun for anyone, even when it works. In real life men can't (or at least don't) always stop themselves from ejaculating in time. 22% of couples trying the withdrawal method end up with a pregnancy in a year.

Rhythm Method: With the rhythm method, the woman tracks her fertility cycle, and the couple avoids intercourse during fertile periods. The rhythm method doesn't work well in practice. A woman may ovulate on an unexpected day. People lose track of the days. About one in four couples using the rhythm method have a pregnancy within a year. The old joke is "What do you call a couple using the rhythm method? Answer: Parents!"

For an added measure of safety, a couple may combine two birth-control methods.

My wife and I really loved using an IUD. It was great because of the ease since she often forgets to take pills.

Latter-day Saint husband, married at 21

We used condoms for a long time because birth control really messed up my emotions, hormones, and emotional state. We both hated that method but did that until we were "done" having children.

—Latter-day Saint wife, married at 22

Sex in Pregnancy

Unless your doctor says otherwise (this will be rare), sex during pregnancy is welcome. Even energetic intercourse does no harm to a growing baby. A couple can have penetrative sex right up to the point the water breaks. A baby is not hurt by the mother's orgasm. Sex does not cause miscarriages.

Orgasm causes muscles to tense. These muscles include the uterus. When a woman isn't pregnant, her uterine contractions aren't visible but may be felt by pressing above her pubic bone. Later in pregnancy, orgasm can trigger a rock-hard uterus for a few minutes. It will subside. A temporarily contracted uterus is safe for the well-cushioned baby.

Still, pregnancy will bring changes to a couple's sex life. A pregnant wife has a changing body with changing hormones. These changes can lead to new and interesting sexual experiences or frustrating ones, depending on the changes and the couple's reaction to the changes.

Sexual desire is hormone driven. As hormones change, sexual appetite may change along with it.

It can be helpful to remember that these changes are outside a wife's control. Some women experience a relative lack of sexual desire during pregnancy. Some pregnant women develop an increased desire for sex. The first trimester, she may be nauseated and find sex unappealing. The third trimester, she may exhausted. Every woman is different. Each pregnancy may be different.

Her body will also change shape and size. A couple can choose to embrace the erotic possibilities of her pregnant body. Doing so may bring a couple closer together during an important stage of marriage. Her physical changes have erotic potential for both husband and wife. A changing body provides sexual novelty. Over the course of pregnancy, her breasts will get larger, and this may be exciting for her to show off and for him to see. Her nipples may become more sensitive. She may find her breast tissue "wants to be touched." Lactation may be earthy and fun. The pregnancy bump may be arousing.

On the other hand, the physical changes of pregnancy may disrupt sex. She may be unhappy with how her body looks and feels. He may not be as visually attracted. Either spouse may find it troubling to think of Mommy as sexy. These feelings may be harmful to her sense of self-worth and may damage the marriage.

A wife's self-confidence should be nurtured. She may need reassurance. A wise practice is for a husband to express sincerely his sexual attraction to his pregnant wife. If he finds her sexually exciting, he should say so. Often. She may believe that stretch marks mar her beauty. He may help her mental state by telling her that stretch marks are symbols of love to him. Openly admiring her physical features that he finds *more* attractive when they are changed by pregnancy can counterbalance negative thoughts she may be having about other body parts.

If a husband finds he is feeling less attracted to his pregnant wife, it can be wise for him to be more attracted by choice. Pregnancy is a good time for a husband to take better control of what turns him on visually. Everyone's body changes over the course of a lifetime. Consciously choosing to remain physically attracted to our spouses through these changes will make our marriages stronger. He can look for the parts that are visually stimulating to him and focus on those. Latter-day Saint men may have learned to keep impure thoughts from dominating the mind by "turning away" when coming across an unwelcome sexual image. He may reverse this process in marriage and "turn towards" his wife. As he fixes sexual imagery of his wife in his memory, this will tend to bond her pregnant form to his mind and his wife to his heart.

This isn't just fun and games. Full commitment is a commandment. Men are commanded in the scriptures to give their all to two—and only two—beings: God and wife. "Thou shalt love thy wife *with all thy heart*, and shalt cleave unto her and none else" (D&C 42:22).

Pregnancy may require physical adjustments for intercourse. Man-on-top may not work very well in the third trimester. A couple may experiment to see what works for them. Different positions may work better later in pregnancy. Woman-on-top, rear entry, scissors, and positions where he stands next to the bed may be comfortable through the late stages of pregnancy.

A man giving his very pregnant wife oral sex may find his neck jammed back by her growing uterus. A pillow placed under her buttocks may make the angle more comfortable for him. She can also try lying on her side—he can use her inner thigh as a pillow and orient his body so his neck is straight.

After the baby is born, the couple will enter a new phase of their sexual life. A wife may not be ready to have sex for several weeks. She will need to heal. Her doctor will give her the medical go-ahead for intercourse during a follow-up visit, typically at four-to-six weeks postpartum. Even with the childbirth trauma healed, sex will not return to normal immediately. Lactation hormones may decrease her libido. She may develop postpartum depression. Most new couples are sleep starved. Both husbands and wives should be understanding if she isn't interested in sex at first. Even after the medical clearance, couples may need to rely on other forms of sexual activity until she finds intercourse to be pleasurable again.

When a wife's body changes, sex changes. These changes may enhance a couple's sex lives or inhibit it. The choice is yours. Choose wisely.

I loved seeing my wife as pregnant. It was a huge turn on.

—Latter-day Saint husband, married at 22

My libido increased. Sex was mostly enjoyable during that time, when I wasn't sick.

—Latter-day Saint wife, married at 22

Misfires

Married sex is a leap of faith. We leap, and we have faith our spouse will catch us. Taking a sexual leap makes us vulnerable—vulnerable to embarrassment, to exposure of our private sexual desires, to shame, and to the answer "no." If we leap, we may fall.

Every couple will have to take leaps of faith for the marriage to thrive sexually. But leaping is only half the act. Spouses also have to catch. Catching can turn a spouse's wild leap into a dance with a thrilling aerial lift. If we don't want our spouse to fall, we have to learn how to catch even if they leap where or when we didn't expect.

One leap of faith is a request for sex. Rejection hurts. Of course, we don't have to agree to sex every time a spouse wants it. What we should do, however, is catch when we can and let a spouse down gently when we cannot.

Catching a spouse who is requesting sex is easier when we answer the right question. The right question is not "am I in the mood?" The right question is "am I willing?" "Am I willing?" sets us up to catch our spouse in the air.

If our answer to "am I willing?" is "not right now," that's okay. When we are not willing to satisfy a request for sex, it's okay to say no...but with tact. We don't want our leaping partner to fall to the ground. We catch. Rather than outright reject, offer a rain check or something to which we would agree now. "I have too much on my plate tonight, but how about Friday morning?" This approach allows the leaping partner to know we will catch...just not this very second. When we offer a rain check, it's best if we are the ones who remember to redeem the check at the agreed-upon time. The rain check allows the leaping spouse to hang still in the air for a bit and build trust in us. Or we might say, "I'm not up for intercourse, but how about a hand job?"

The leaping spouse should accept with grace a rain check or an offer of something different but still sexual. Doing otherwise can lead to duty sex and resentment.

Sometimes a spouse may leap by requesting a new sexual activity. The leaping partner would do well to time requests for sex novelty strategically. There are good times and there are bad times to ask for something new in the bedroom. A good time to ask to try something new is when a couple is already being a bit sexual. Arousal helps lower inhibitions to the new. An aroused spouse is more likely to catch.

What if our answer to "am I willing?" to try something new in the bedroom is "HARD no. Not now. Not ever."? It's okay if we have to say "no." Sometimes we find sexual acts to be too taboo.

Sometimes we have deeply held convictions. Sometimes we refuse because of trauma. Whatever the reason, the rejection should be done with great tact. Rejection comes with our spouse's worry that we find the request to be disgusting or our spouse to be perverted. As the one saying "no," we can allay our spouse's anxieties. "I'm flattered you'd want to do that with me. I'm so honored you would entrust me with that. I have to tell you that I really don't think that's something I can do. Even though I don't think I can do what you want in this way, I love everything about you, even this. Instead, why don't we try...?" We catch each other in the kindest way we can.

The most important tool in the married couple's sexual toolkit may be kindness. This kindness extends to the self and the spouse. Kindness also catches a spouse during sexual misfires.

Mortal bodies are not 100% reliable. Erections, arousal, and orgasms don't always come to pass. Misfires will happen. Be kind. A couple's reaction to sexual misfires can make the difference between an "oops" moment and lasting trauma. That trauma comes when a sexual misfire is taken to mean something it does not—he doesn't love me; she doesn't find me attractive; whatever. Kindness helps occasional misfires remain just that: misfires.

Misfires are going to happen. It's important to remember that a misfire may not mean anything. Occasional misfires are normal and do not imply the body needs treatment or the marriage is in jeopardy. If a wife finds it difficult to orgasm one night, that may not mean she doesn't like sex or that her husband is a bad lover. If he has erectile dysfunction from time to time, that doesn't mean he doesn't find his wife attractive or is a failure as a man.

Misfires don't traumatize a marriage. Unkind reactions to misfires traumatize a marriage. "Can't get it up? What's wrong with you?" can traumatize a husband. "What the heck is taking you so long?" can traumatize a wife. And so on. An unkind word can take a lifetime to heal. We are all so vulnerable during sex.

This extends to self-talk. "Am I broken?" is not a sexy thought. It is vitally important to a marriage that a couple turn toward each other for emotional support following sexual misfires. It may feel easier to withdraw from a spouse after a sexual misfire. Some people walk out of the bedroom in embarrassment over a misfire. Some people start to avoid sex so the misfire never happens again. This withdrawal can bewilder a spouse. The shame and confusion over what a misfire supposedly means can fracture a marriage.

With kindness, a couple may walk away from sexual misfires bonded by the experience. For this to work, we have to trust our spouses to be kind after a misfire, and we must worthy of our spouse's trust.

Some sexual misfires are to be expected, and some may need treatment. There is a sexual equivalent to the ten-second rule when you drop food on the floor. The misfire rule is one month. Any misfire that goes away in a month doesn't count. A temporary sexual misfire is unlikely to have an underlying cause other than the imperfection of the mortal body.

If a misfire hits the one-month mark of happening consistently, it's time to get to the bottom of things. Persistent misfires usually benefit from treatment. For the marriage to thrive, persistent sexual misfires should be addressed.

Most Common Female Misfires

Orgasm may be difficult for a woman to learn if she hasn't had one prior to marriage. This is normal. Sexual activity without orgasm can be exciting and enjoyable for her while she and her husband are figuring out sex together. If she is receiving adequate stimulation and does not experience orgasm within a month of regular sexual activity, she may benefit from sex therapy. Success rates are A-grade high (95%) with treatment through directed self-exploration.

Sex therapists who serve Latter-day Saint couples are likely to discuss treatment with the couple together. A wife's directed self-exploration as part of couples therapy is not a secret hidden from her husband. Most often a Latter-day Saint husband yearns for his wife to experience orgasm and is enthusiastic about her doing whatever it takes for her to learn about her body's sexual potential.

A wife may need to develop her sexuality on her own a bit before it's possible for her to share it with her husband. She may bless her marriage by learning how her body works and how to orgasm. She will be able to bring what she has learned back to the marriage bed. She can show her husband what touches work for her and share her orgasmic potential with him.

The most successful method of treatment will have the wife understand her anatomy and explore her body. The focus will be on her trying different types of touch (fast, slow, light, firm) and noticing what sensations each touch brings. This isn't arousal oriented but an exploration where she attends to how her body responds to different touches without judgment. She will be directed first to try nongenital touch then genital touch. After she learns what touches are pleasurable, her therapist will direct her to arouse her body with genital touch or a vibrator. If a prolonged application of a vibrator (an hour) does not lead to her first orgasm, she may be worked up medically to rule out medical causes. Vibrators work.

Some Latter-day Saint wives are uncomfortable with the thought of self-exploration even while they understand that her orgasm would bless the marriage. It may help if her therapist explains that it may be more difficult for her to relax with her husband in the room during her self-exploration. Being observed can be stressful. It may be too exposing to be watched while learning pleasurable touch. If self-exploration is too taboo for her to try—or if she just prefers things that way—she may choose to have her husband serve as her hands.

Once a wife has learned to orgasm, it's not going to be automatic every time. Some nights, even experienced couples find that orgasm isn't happening for her. When things get to the point of chafing, patience is unlikely to get her there.

Some "solve" this problem by faking orgasm. We suggest you never do this. A husband cannot learn how to recognize the signs of things progressing if his wife pretends. He may never learn what she needs if he's told the wrong way was right.

A husband has to be okay with his wife not having an orgasm if she says it's not working out this time. It's not a failure. Instead, he may consider it an investment. A lovemaking session where she doesn't climax may make her more primed for an orgasm next time...if he's cool about it. On the other hand, putting pressure on her about having an orgasm can be a huge turn off and may have her consider faking it just to get him to back the heck off. A husband should be a considerate lover. This includes being respectful if his wife doesn't want an orgasm this time or wants to stop trying for now.

Most Common Male Misfires

At the other end of the orgasmic spectrum, sometimes a man will ejaculate when he doesn't want. This may happen while he is giving his wife pleasure. Her sexual arousal will arouse him. He may, from time to time, find that pleasuring his wife is all a bit too exciting. He may ejaculate before he wants. This is worth talking through as a couple.

If a husband senses he's about to ejaculate while he is pleasuring his wife, what does she want? Does she want him to stop what he's doing, receive an orgasm from intercourse or other stimulation, and get back to pleasuring her? He's likely to go along with that plan if that works for her.

If the wife wants her husband to attend to her pleasure rather than stop in the middle, that's perfectly understandable. If she finds it flattering to know he finds her so exciting he loses control, she should let him know that. That knowledge will free him up to let her know he's about to orgasm. On the other hand, if she finds his ejaculation distracting, he may wish conceal it until she has climaxed.

About one in three men complain about being unable to delay orgasm during intercourse. Premature ejaculation is the most common male sexual complaint. The typical man ejaculates after five minutes of intercourse. Just knowing the five-minute number helps some men realize they are perfectly normal. Occasional rapid ejaculation is also normal.

For ejaculation to qualify clinically as "premature," three things must be true. The ejaculation must be (1) within one minute of vaginal insertion, (2) nearly every time, and (3) unwanted.

If the couple finds the husband's rapid ejaculation to be persistent and distressing, there are bedroom exercises that may help. A professional is likely to recommend behavioral therapy. These behavioral techniques empower him with the start of control over his orgasm. Control leads to confidence. With growing confidence, he may relax during intercourse. Relaxation will give him even more control in a virtuous circle.

Two at-home techniques for practicing orgasmic control are start-stop and squeeze.

The start-stop technique is what it sounds like. The couple begins a sexual encounter that would normally stimulate him to orgasm. When the husband realizes he is approaching orgasm, the couple stops and waits for his excitement to subside before continuing. Doing this four or five times in a row may help develop his control and confidence. Over time he should learn to extend his plateau phase and sense his approach to his orgasmic point of no return.

The second orgasmic control practice technique is squeeze. The squeeze technique was first developed by the sex researchers Masters and Johnson. As in the start-stop technique, the couple starts sexual activity that would normally bring the husband to the brink. He tells his wife when he is nearing orgasm. The couple stops what they are doing. She squeezes the area where the tip of his penis meets the shaft pretty darn firmly. It won't work if he does it. It has to be her. The squeeze causes him a bit of discomfort. She holds the squeeze until he says it's safe. The couple repeats several times before allowing him to orgasm.

A variation on the start-stop and squeeze techniques adds a bit of intercourse in the woman-on-top position (so the husband can be as relaxed as possible). He shouldn't move. The idea is to let him experience the sensation of penetration and his wife thrusting once or twice without his having an orgasm. This exercise lets him experience intercourse where his orgasm isn't uncontrollable.

Perhaps the simplest home treatment for premature ejaculation is for the husband to have an orgasm prior to intercourse. Assuming he is able to achieve an erection after an orgasm, he will likely have greater orgasmic control after a first orgasm.

Condoms lessen penile sensation and may help. There are even over-the-counter control condoms with a topical anesthetic.

Another common male sexual misfire is erectile dysfunction. If a husband approaches a month of being unable to sustain an erection most of the time, he should seek professional help.

Persistent sexual misfires can have eternal consequences if untreated. Seeking help is the hard part. Most sexual misfires are easy to treat.

I wish I had known about premature ejaculation.
—Latter-day Saint husband, married at 22

It took more than two years into our marriage to have an orgasm because I was clueless. My poor husband just wanted me to feel the same pleasure and release.
—Latter-day Saint wife, married at 20

When to Call a Professional

There are some sexual ailments that need medical treatment. Some need a counselor or sex therapist. Some go away on their own. Some can wait for your next check-up. Some are emergencies.

We've already talked about the one-month rule for misfires. You may find yourself wondering if you should reach for the phone for other sexual ailments, especially on your wedding night. This list is not exhaustive. If you have questions, call your physician. You should always feel comfortable asking your doctor about any concerns you have about sex. If your doctor is unable or unwilling to answer—or is clueless—ask another doctor.

Bleeding

If a wife has severe bleeding, call a physician immediately. This may be a medical emergency. Spotting or light vaginal bleeding after first intercourse is normal. A newlywed wife may bleed for a few days after the wedding night. Any post-sex bleeding that continues for more than a few days, even if the bleeding is light, should be checked out by a physician. After about a week following first intercourse, she should not bleed after sex. If she does, she should consult her physician. A pregnant woman with vaginal bleeding should contact her doctor immediately.

Pain

Occasional discomfort is normal. Pain is not. If it's painful, something is wrong. Sex should never be painful. Don't suffer in silence. A painful experience leads to anxiety and more pain. Stop what you are doing so things don't get worse. The most common cause of intercourse pain is insufficient lubrication. This is easily remedied. If the pain is more than a one-time experience, a couple should seek medical attention. If a health-care provider does not appear to be addressing a wife's pain adequately, she should request a referral to a pelvic pain specialist.

Urinary Tract Infections

UTIs are common in women. Symptoms include more frequent urination, burning urination, pelvic pain, and urine that is cloudy, pink, cola-colored, or strong-smelling. A woman's urethra is short, so sex can introduce bacteria into her bladder. First sexual intercourse, or even first sex with a new partner, may lead to a UTI.

UTIs can be made less probable if the wife drinks plenty of water and urinates after intercourse to flush out bacteria. She should not douche. Douching may cause UTIs. Drinking cranberry juice may help prevent UTIs. She should call her doctor if she has the signs of a UTI.

Vaginismus

Vaginismus probably won't happen to you, but if it does, you'll want to know what it is and what you should do.

It's not uncommon for women to have an involuntary tightening of the vagina. This can be overcome by using fingers to stretch the vagina and overcome the reflex. In a small number of women, the involuntary reflex is strong and is called vaginismus. The vagina clamps shut and prevents intercourse. Some have compared vaginismus to an eye blinking when something pokes it.

The wedding night is the most common occasion for a woman to experience vaginismus. One anonymous Latter-day Saint bride described it this way online: "I bawled on my wedding night. And not the pretty 'I'm so happy right now' kind of tears....We couldn't make anything work."

Vaginismus is distressing, as you might expect.

Vaginismus has physical and psychological components. If the wife is afraid of sex or if she believes sex to be sinful, vaginismus is more likely. Reading this book before the honeymoon may help. If she can embrace the goodness of her sexuality and look forward to intercourse after her husband gives her ample foreplay, the odds of vaginismus drop. That said, even women who welcome sex may experience vaginismus and find even tampons impossible to insert.

The standard treatment for vaginismus is touch therapy, where the woman will touch herself near her vagina and train her muscles to relax until she can insert a finger without pain. She may be prescribed vaginal dilators to stretch her vagina.

Vaginismus is not forever. Most women with vaginismus report pain-free intercourse within five weeks.

Sexually Transmitted Infections

STIs may be undiagnosed and asymptomatic. STIs sometimes are discovered when a sexual partner develops symptoms. If you suspect you or your spouse has an STI, you should seek medical advice and treatment. Untreated STIs may cause permanent damage, including infertility. Signs of potential STIs (outside general infection symptoms) may include painful or burning urination, discharge from the penis, abnormal or odd-smelling vaginal discharge, swollen lymph nodes near the groin, and genital sores or bumps. If you have an STI, your spouse is going to find out about it sooner or later. Spouses must be honest about their STI history. STIs don't go away if you ignore them. If you try to hide an STI, things will get *much* worse.

Erectile Dysfunction

Occasional ED is normal. Persistent ED may benefit from psychological or medical treatment.

If a man is consistently having trouble achieving or keeping an erection or finds it more difficult over time, this may be a sign of a medical problem. He can call his doctor if he's concerned. He may be treated with an ED drug that increases blood flow. Viagra, the first ED drug, was discovered by accident when a pill being tested for chest pain caused erections as a side effect. "You know, doctor, there was this one other thing that happened during the trial...."

Pharmaceuticals have revolutionized the treatment of ED. However, not all ED has a medical cause. If a man has persistent trouble with erections during sex but wakes up with an erection or can achieve an erection through self-stimulation, there may be a psychological cause to his ED. A sex therapist may help address psychological causes of ED.

Premature Ejaculation

We discussed premature ejaculation in the "Misfires" chapter. If premature ejaculation happens nearly every time for a month, a couple may benefit from professional advice. It may help to see a sex therapist, who will be able to guide the couple through behavioral techniques and help reduce the husband's anxiety. A medical doctor may prescribe an antidepressant to lower the man's ability to experience orgasm. A doctor may also prescribe a topical anesthetic, tramadol, or an ED drug, often in combination with behavioral therapy.

Low Libido

Sexual-desire differences in a marriage are normal. What one spouse may believe to be low desire may be a perfectly normal desire difference.

Sometimes a lack of desire has a medical or psychological basis that may be treated. Anyone who lacks sexual thoughts and desires and finds that lack to be distressing may wish to seek professional advice.

It's important to note that low libido is currently most treatable medically when there is something obvious to correct. A medical doctor may look for an underlying medical condition to treat or a medication to change. For example, some antidepressants interfere with libido and ability to experience orgasm in both men and women. If you believe antidepressants may be interfering with your sexual satisfaction, you should consult your doctor for a potential medication switch or add-on medication that may temper the unwanted side effects.

A medical doctor may prescribe a woman the drug Addyi to treat low desire.

It's possible some birth-control hormones interfere with a woman's libido. Most studies show no effect, and more studies show increased libido from hormonal birth control overall. Each woman is different though. She may ask her doctor to consider switching her to a different birth-control method if hormonal birth control may be interfering with her libido.

When there is no obvious medical cause to resolve, medical doctors will have nothing to treat. A sex therapist or counselor may be helpful in identifying and addressing psychological causes for low libido once obvious medical causes have been ruled out.

Sex is used to bind the relationship, so treatment helps solidify that bond when necessary. It's like a house, sometimes the faucet won't work properly so you need to make some repairs to get it functioning.
—Latter-day Saint husband, married at 23

It doesn't always have anything to do with you, your partner, or how much you love each other. Sometimes, there are medical issues that can cause problems that are otherwise invisible or that you don't realize have impacts on your sex life.
—Latter-day Saint husband, married at 27

Game Night Trivia

Knowing what is normal isn't always helpful. What's normal for one couple would be deeply frustrating to another. When it comes to sex, it really doesn't much matter what normal is for the group if it's not normal for the couple. Still...we all kind of want to know. Plus, knowing what's normal can be liberating for some of us.

How often do married couples have sex?

Before we blurt out the answer, let's talk about the Goldilocks effect. Sex frequency can be "too hot," "too cold," or "just right." Couples that have sex less often than once a week report lower happiness ("too cold"). Couples that have sex at least once a week report the highest happiness ("just right"). Couples who have sex more than once a week ("too hot") report the same happiness as the sex-once-a-week couples.

Some couples try a sex-every-day-for-a-month experiment. Results are mixed. Most couples report feeling closer. Most couples also find it hard to keep to the schedule. So go figure.

Sex seems to be like money. Not enough can make you miserable. Enough is enough. More than enough doesn't make you happier. Whatever works for the couple is obviously fine.

So what do most married couples do? Too hot? Too cold? Just right? The average married couple in the United States has sex about once per week.

Just right.

How many women orgasm?

Almost all women (about 95%) eventually learn to orgasm.

How many women orgasm in intercourse?

Only one in four women reports climaxing consistently from intercourse...plus direct clitoral stimulation, usually. About half of women sometimes orgasm during intercourse. One in five women *never* climaxes during intercourse. Whatever the woman experiences, she has a lot of company.

How many orgasms can a woman have?

About half of women report they may have multiple orgasms in one session of continual vibrator stimulation. We note this result selects for women who use vibrators in this way, and the true average may be different.

About 8% of women report they experience multiple orgasms easily via sex that includes intercourse. About 11%-12% of women report multiple orgasms from their most recent intercourse.

Some women can have an apparently unlimited number of orgasms in a row—this has been documented under laboratory conditions. Extreme examples are women with a rare pathology of being constantly aroused who find they are driven to stimulate themselves to orgasm hundreds of times each day. This is not as fun as it sounds, by the way. Women with this condition tend to be depressed and feel cursed.

This is all to say that multiple orgasms are not a myth. It's important to note that many women do not experience multiple orgasms and also report high satisfaction with sexual activity.

How big is an average penis?

To measure a penis properly, it must be erect. A ruler is placed on top until it hits the man's pubic bone. The average penis size in the US is...5.1 inches.

Now that we have that out of the way, penis size *really* doesn't matter to most women. In survey after survey, most women say they don't care. They are the experts. A penis doesn't provide much stimulation to a woman during intercourse. There are a few women who do prefer very large penises, but these women are in the minority. The most common reaction women give when they are asked about large penises is that too big can be painful.

FYI, no nutritional supplement has been shown to increase penis size, so save your money, men.

To shave or not to shave?

It's currently popular in some cultures to shave pubic hair. Some couples like the shaved look. Shaving has a cost and not just in multi-blade razors and ingrown hairs. Our heavenly parents put pubic hair there for a reason. Pubic hair wicks moisture away from the genitals and prevents chafing. A shaved pubis is not cleaner. There is no physical reason to shave pubic hair.

Never blow air in a vagina

Air in a vagina can cause an embolism, a dangerous bubble where it shouldn't be. An embolism can kill a woman if the air enters her bloodstream. This is more likely when she is pregnant because of increased vulval blood supply. Don't blow air into the vagina at any time but especially not during pregnancy. That doesn't mean all air is dangerous in a vagina. A small bit of air can sometimes get trapped inadvertently. This can happen during sex. The air will come out with an airy fart noise called a queef. This is normal.

Don't douche

A woman's vagina cleans itself. Douching is not necessary and may lead to infections.

Menstruation is no reason to avoid sex

In the *Old Testament*, bleeding women were considered unclean. We know better. Sex during a period is safe and natural. Orgasm may relieve a wife's menstrual cramps. She will need to remove any tampon before intercourse, of course. You may want to put down a towel if she is a heavy bleeder. Some couples may find intercourse during menstruation to be a turn-off. These couples may consider other modes of sexual activity during her time of the month.

69 is not a lucky number

The 69 position is mutual oral sex where one spouse has his or her head toward the other's feet. Each spouse gives oral sex to the other at the same time. This can be erotic. However, 69 is probably no more than an interesting appetizer instead of a real meal for most couples. Most women report the 69 position to be too distracting for them to reach orgasm.

Orgasm is possible after spinal cord injury

Spinal cord injuries are not the end of an active sex life. There are erogenous zones outside the genitals that may become more sexually sensitive. In fact, about half of those who have complete transection of the spinal cord may still be able to orgasm. Orgasm is in the brain.

In women, stimulation from the clitoris travels through the pelvic and pudendal nerves. Sensation through these nerves may indeed be blocked by spinal cord injury. However, another nerve, the vagus nerve, does not pass through the spinal cord. The vagus nerve passes outside the spinal cord through the neck into the trunk. Parts of the vagus nerve access the uterus and the cervix. About half of women with spinal cord injuries are able to orgasm through cervical and deep vaginal stimulation.

Women with spinal cord injuries may desire or require more nipple stimulation to reach orgasm. Very nearly the same regions in the brain light up with clitoral, vaginal, and nipple stimulation.

A typical erection is initiated from the brain, and spinal cord injuries tend to sever this most common pathway to erection. A second type of erection is triggered from direct stimulation and may be possible after spinal cord injury. One or both of orgasm and ejaculation may be possible, depending on the location of the spinal cord injury.

I wish we would have been more willing to communicate our desires instead of being shy.
—Latter-day Saint husband, married at 23

Things taught by my parents as "church doctrine" were their own convictions not actually the church's stance.
—Latter-day Saint wife, married at 20

Zion

We asked the Latter-day Saints who responded to our wedding-night survey to tell us how their sex lives improved over the course of marriage. We asked, "If you wanted to let a new Latter-day Saint couple know how good sex can be, what would you tell them? In your own experience, what is the thing you have found to be most joyful about sex?" Their answers give a window into what married sex can be with time and experience.

Multiple couples cited the joy of learning about each other's bodies and their own. "It gets better" is a theme.

There's a learning curve. I love that you learn together with your spouse.
—*Latter-day Saint wife, married at 21*

Sex with someone that you get to know and try different things with only gets better and better.
—*Latter-day Saint husband, married at 27*

It might take some time before you are satisfied with the sexual aspect of your relationship. Sometimes it takes time to learn selflessness and healthy communication skills. Don't be discouraged if things

aren't perfect in the beginning. Just be patient with one another and enjoy the process of learning and growing together.
                    —Latter-day Saint wife, married at 22

Communication is key. It took us about six months to be truly honest about our needs, emotions, and expectations. And that experimentation is good within the limits we defined. That took about a year.
                    —Latter-day Saint wife, married at 21

Sex has gotten much better as our marriage has gone on and on. The things that have helped me the most have been for me to learn that I should not be manipulative in the way I try to get my wife to have sex with me. That has helped us a lot.
                    —Latter-day Saint husband, married at 21

It's okay to laugh and enjoy. It took nine months or so before we relaxed.
                    —Latter-day Saint husband, married at 26

It gets easier and less awkward with time. It's unfair to expect to know how to pleasure your spouse right off the bat. You'll learn what you and your spouse like, and it'll be so much more enjoyable when you get to that point. Married sex has so much more meaning to me than what the world wants you to think about sex. It's the most intimate way of expressing love, and it's fun at the same time.
                    —Latter-day Saint wife, married at 24

Learning new things can be uncomfortable. A bit of discomfort is what we all feel until we master something new. But learning is required for growth and maturity. Sexual learning does not come just from reading books. Learning about sexuality necessarily employs the body in unfamiliar ways. Unfamiliar sexual activities make us all uncomfortable at first.

Keep an open mind. It's impossible to know exactly what you might enjoy sexually until you try it. When you were in the first grade, kissing probably seemed icky. Kissing may have been awkward the first time you tried it. But you did try it and found you liked it with the right person at the right time. Now you wouldn't think of going without it. Learning new things allows a couple to maximize their callings as sexual beings.

Latter-day Saint couples rave about the emotional connection of married sex. There is a oneness that comes from it. The strength of the sexual connection in marriage is surprising even to those who were unsurprised by the physicality of sex. Sex forges a sacred bond, the power of which can be sensed. We know as Latter-day Saints that the bond can be eternal. You will feel it.

> *The most joyful thing about married sex is how connected we feel as a couple. It's very unifying, loving, and happy.*
> —Latter-day Saint wife, married at 21

> *The emotional connection and spiritual power of the act is almost unbelievable if done in humility, holiness, and honesty.*
> —Latter-day Saint husband, married at 26

> *I would tell them how wonderful it is to feel that sacred bond with your spouse. That sex isn't about the physical. It's about the emotional part. And that it's so much better when you're honest and open with your partner about your expectations like how*

much you want to go or what feels good to you.
—Latter-day Saint wife, married at 21

I would tell them that it's great and feels good physically but that the emotional connection and emotions in general related to sex are very intense.... Don't underestimate the emotions involved. The most enjoyable is the closeness I experience and, of course, the physical reaction.
—Latter-day Saint husband, married at 22

Before marriage (during the engagement), my husband and I explored our bodies a little together. Although we never felt guilty about it, sex after marriage felt "right." That's the only explanation I have.
—Latter-day Saint wife, married at 21

It makes me feel connected to my wife and that I can face the world because my wife is in my corner.
—Latter-day Saint husband, married at 22

I would tell them that they can feel the most pleasure they have ever felt and at the same time feel more connected to the person that they love than they ever have
—Latter-day Saint husband, married at 23

Sex is for both of you. Some things will come easier, but the most important thing is to communicate and listen.
—Latter-day Saint husband, married at 23

I would tell them about the utter vulnerability of it all. It seems strange for somebody who hasn't felt it yet. It's...the sense of oneness that comes in. In those moments, it's you and your spouse and nothing else. The experience brings you closer in a way I never thought possible before.
—Latter-day Saint husband, married at 23

Most joyful: connecting with your spouse as you are both vulnerable and completely open to each other, getting a release of tension together and falling asleep naked (this is an important part of sex—don't jump up and put your temple garments back on right away).
—Latter-day Saint wife, married at 22

The intimacy of the emotional connection is amazing. Also, it can feel so. Freaking. Good.
—Latter-day Saint wife, married at 34

The oneness of sex is borne of acceptance. Each of us needs to know we are acceptable—an acceptable wife, an acceptable husband. All people yearn to hear how attractive they are, how talented they are, and how loved they are.

When it comes to sex, only you can do this for your spouse. Is your spouse sexually attractive to you? Say so. Is your spouse sexually talented? Express wonder at that talent. Do you love sex with your spouse? Give thanks. Fill your spouse's soul with words they have waited a lifetime to hear. Build them up and become one. With that oneness, you can turn and face the world together. With that oneness, you may move together through time and all eternity.

Sex will not only draw you two together. Sex will bring you both closer to God. As you participate in the procreative act, you will join in an essential part of God's work and glory. Through sex, you will participate more fully in God's plan of happiness. Should your bodies allow, with the power of sex you will raise children of your own flesh. Even should your bodies not allow, you may be a full partner with God through your willingness to carry out his very first commandment: Have sex.

> THE FIRST COMMANDMENT that God gave to Adam and Eve pertained to their potential for parenthood as husband and wife. We declare that God's commandment for His children to multiply and replenish the earth remains in force. We further declare that God has commanded that the sacred powers of procreation are to be employed only between man and woman, lawfully wedded as husband and wife.
>
> —The Family: A Proclamation to the World

And it is very good.

EARTHLY PARENTS

We always viewed it as a gift to be opened when appropriate.

—Latter-day Saint wife, married at 21

We are sexual beings and sex is FUN. So take a deep breath and enjoy it.

—Latter-day Saint wife, married at 23

Sources

General Reference

Bechtel, S. and R. Stains. *Sex: A Man's Guide.* Rodale Press. 1996.

Finlayson-Fife, J. Ask the Mormon Sex Therapist (series). *Rational Faiths* (podcast).

Joannides, P. *Guide to Getting It On.* 5th ed. Goofy Foot Press. 2006.

Nagoski, E. *Come As You Are: The Surprising New Science that Will Transform Your Sex Life.* Simon and Schuster Paperbacks. 2015.

Parker, N. *Mormon Sex Info* (podcast)

Parker, N. *The Mormon Therapist* (blog). patheos.com/blogs/mormontherapist/

Watson L. and A. Mathews. *Foreplay Radio Sex Therapy.* (podcast)

Westheimer, R., et al. *Sex for Dummies.* 3rd ed. For Dummies Press. 2006.

Sexual Attitudes of Latter-day Saints

Finlayson-Fife, J. Female Sexual Agency in

Patriarchal Culture: The Case of Mormon Women. PhD dissertation. Boston College. 2002.

Mackelprang, R. "'And They Shall Be One Flesh': Sexuality and Contemporary Mormonism." *Dialogue*. 1992. 25(1). 49–67.

Dual-control Model of Sexual Arousal
Janssen, E. and J. Bancroft. "The Dual Control Model: The Role of Sexual Inhibition and Excitation in Sexual Arousal and Behavior." In Janssen E. (ed). *The Psychophysiology of Sex*. Indiana University Press. 2007. 197–222.

Structure of the Clitoris
O'Connell H., et al. "Anatomy of the Clitoris." *Journal of Urology*. 2005. 174(4 Pt 1): 1189–1195.

Sexual Scenes (Fantasies)
Friday, N. My Secret Garden: Women's Sexual Fantasies. Trident Press. 1973.

Lehmiller, J. Tell Me What You Want: The Science of Sexual Desire and How It Can Help You Improve Your Sex Life. Da Capo Press. 2018.

Marriage Heat (website). marriageheat.com. Note: A Latter-day Saint sex therapist who reviewed this book prior to print recommends this site for member clients seeking ideas for a wife's sexual scenes. The website compiles erotica written from a married Christian perspective.

Share of Women Who Orgasm and How
Herbenick D., et al. "Women's Experiences with Genital Touching, Sexual Pleasure, and Orgasm: Results From a U.S. Probability Sample of Women

Ages 18 to 94." *Journal of Sex and Marital Therapy.* 2018. 44(2): 201–212.

Lloyd, E. The Case of the Female Orgasm: Bias in the Science of Evolution. Harvard University Press. 2005.

Sex Frequency of Married American Couples

Twenge J., et al. "Declines in Sexual Frequency among American Adults." *Archives of Sexual Behavior.* 2017. 46(8): 2389–2401.

Sex Frequency and Happiness

Muise A., et al. "Sexual Frequency Predicts Greater Well-being, but More Is Not Always Better." *Social Psychological and Personality Science.* 2016. 7(4). 295–302.

Importance of Cuddling After Sex

Muise, A., et al. "Post-sex Affectionate Exchanges Promote Sexual and Relationship Satisfaction." *Archives of Sexual Behavior.* 2018. 43:1391–1402.

Sex in Pregnancy

www.mayoclinic.org/healthy-lifestyle/labor-and-delivery/in-depth/sex-after-pregnancy/art-20045669

www.mayoclinic.org/healthy-lifestyle/pregnancy-week-by-week/in-depth/sex-during-pregnancy/art-20045318

Birth Control

Division of Reproductive Health, National Center for Chronic Disease Prevention and Health Promotion, Centers for Disease Control and Prevention. "Selected Practice Recommendations for Contraceptive Use, 2013." *MMWR Recommendations and Reports.* 2013. 62(5): 1–60.

Trussell, J. "Contraceptive Efficacy." In Hatcher R et al. (ed). *Contraceptive Technology.* 20th revised ed. Ardent Media. 2011. 779–863.

Trussell, J. "Contraceptive Failure in the United States." *Contraception.* 2011. 83(5): 397–404.

When to Call a Professional

health.clevelandclinic.org/what-should-you-do-if-you-bleed-after-sex/

www.mayoclinic.org/diseases-conditions/sexually-transmitted-diseases-stds/symptoms-causes/syc-20351240

www.mayoclinic.org/diseases-conditions/urinary-tract-infection/symptoms-causes/syc-20353447

www.merckmanuals.com/home/women-s-health-issues/sexual-dysfunction-in-women/vaginismus

www.webmd.com/erectile-dysfunction/guide/understanding-erectile-dysfunction-symptoms

Orgasm After Spinal Cord Injury

Komisaruk, B., et al. "Brain Activation during Vaginocervical Self-stimulation and Orgasm in Women with Complete Spinal Cord Injury: fMRI Evidence of Mediation by the Vagus Nerves." *Brain Research.* 2004. 1024(1–2): 77–88.

Sipski, M., et al. "Effects of Level and Degree of Spinal Cord Injury on Male Orgasm." *Spinal Cord.* 2006. 44: 798–804.

Sipski, M., et al. "Sexual Arousal and Orgasm in Women: Effects of Spinal Cord Injury." *Annals of Neurology.* 2001. 49(1): 35–44.

We thank Natasha Helfer Parker, Romel Mackelprang, and Jennifer Finlayson-Fife for reviewing drafts of the manuscript and providing insights from the perspective of sex therapists who treat Latter-day Saint couples. Your help made the book better. Thank you.

A practical, forthright guide to marital sexuality. **And It Was Very Good** *offers important sex education and relationship guidance that many Latter-day Saint couples need.*
—*Jennifer Finlayson-Fife, PhD, LCPC*
Host of the "Ask a Mormon Sex Therapist" podcast.

And It Was Very Good *is a valuable resource of clinically accurate and comprehensive sexual education that fits within the value structure of Latter-day Saints. Many problems I see as a sex therapist could be avoided if couples had this type of information prior to or at the beginning of their marital relationship.*
—*Natasha Helfer Parker, LCMFT, CST*
Host of the "Mormon Sex Info" podcast.

A comprehensive resource for couples to help navigate the landscape of sexual intimacy within marriage. I'm glad there are more resources out there for couples (and for parents!). I would even refer this book to clients who are not of our faith.
—*Barbara Murray, MSW, LCSW*
Author of Taking Back Parenting

And It Was Very Good *is by far the most helpful book I have read on how to have healthy sex and make love with your spouse. It gives couples a mature and responsible view of marital sex as well as paving the way to help couples avoid sexual neglect and dormant passion that thrives in too many marriages.*
—*Elaine J. Davis, LPC, LMFT*

I became a marriage and family therapist in part to share what I have learned from my own mistakes, and give others hope. Reading your book makes me wish I had had it before I got married!
—*Kelley Molinari, LMFTA*

What a great guide for couples wanting to expand on their intimate relationship. Most religious based sexual education books gloss over intimacy, but **And It Was Very Good** goes in depth, which can help couples have the much needed conversations to improve their intimate relationship.

—Dena LeTendre, LCMHC

I have read every LDS book on sex and nothing has come close to being this helpful.

—Matthew Bridgstock, LCSW, CST, CSA

As a parent of young children and a marriage and family therapist, I find **And It Was Very Good** profoundly useful in both my personal and professional lives.

—Caitlin Olsen, MS, LMFT

A practical, easy read guide in helping couples maneuver through delicate issues without feeling embarrassed or inadequate.

—Trevor Irish, LCMHC

And It Was Very Good provides practical information about sex for married heterosexual couples in a safe and tasteful framework that many Latter-day Saints will appreciate and find non-threatening. If you would like to know more about sexuality but would prefer to avoid internet searches and pornographic material, this book is for you.

—Kelly Furr, MS, LAMFT

Our Family's
SEXUAL ARTICLES OF FAITH

— ❧ —

*W*E BELIEVE SEXUALITY is a good gift from our heavenly parents.

2 We believe married sex is for joy and bonding in addition to creating new mortal bodies for spirit children to inhabit.

3 We believe God ordained sex for the married couple. Nobody else should be involved.

4 We believe sex is not a right to be demanded but a gift to be offered and received voluntarily.

5 We believe husbands and wives are individually responsible for expressing their own sexual desires and for caring for each other's sexual needs.

6 We believe viewing pornography is forbidden.

7 We believe sex that unites a married couple in Christ is good and sex that divides a married couple is bad.

EARTHLY PARENTS

Made in the USA
Las Vegas, NV
02 December 2022

61017541R00105